# Action Learning and Action Research Journal

## Vol 26 No 2 December 2020

*Action Learning, Action Research Association Ltd (and its predecessors) has published the ALAR Journal since 1996.*

**Managing Editor:** Prof. Mishack Gumbo
University of South Africa

**Issue Editor:** Prof. Mishack Gumbo

**Global Strategic Editorial Board:**
Dr Azril Bacal, University of Uppsala, Sweden
Dr Susan Goff, Murray-Darling Basin Authority, Australia
A/Prof Erik Lindhult, Mälardalen University, Sweden
Riripeti Reedy, Ngati Porou, Director, Maitai Group Ltd, New Zealand
Prof Shankar Sankaran, University of Technology Sydney, Australia
Dr Shawn Wilson, Southern Cross University, Australia

**Editorial inquiries:**
The Editor, *ALAR Journal*
Action Learning, Action Research Association Ltd
PO Box 162, Greenslopes, Qld 4120 Australia

editor@alarassociation.org

ISSN 1326-964X (Print)   ISSN 2206-611X (Online)

The Action Learning and Action Research Journal is listed in:
- Australian Research Council – *Excellence in Research for Australia (ERA) 2018 Journal List*
- Australian Business Deans Council *2019 ABDC Journal Quality List*

# Editorial Advisory Board

| | |
|---|---|
| Assoc. Prof. Chivonne Algeo | Australia |
| Dr Noa Avriel-Avni | Israel |
| Dr Paul Aylward | Australia |
| Dr Gina Blackberry | Australia |
| Dr Graeme Brown | Australia |
| Dr Pip Bruce Ferguson | New Zealand |
| Dr Deeanna Burleson | USA |
| Dr Ross Colliver | Australia |
| Mr Andrew Cook | Australia |
| Ms Maya Cordeiro | Australia |
| Dr Philip Crane | Australia |
| Dr Karen Crinall | Australia |
| Capt Michael Dent | Malaysia |
| Dr Bob Dick | Australia |
| Dr Stephen Duffield | Australia |
| Dr Wayne Fallon | Australia |
| Dr Susan Goff | Australia |
| Assoc. Prof. Marina Harvey | Australia |
| Dr Geof Hill | Australia |
| Ms Jane Holloway | Australia |
| Dr Ernest Hughes | USA |
| Dr Angela James | South Africa |
| Dr Brian Jennings | Ghana |
| Dr Jaime Jimenez-Guzman | Mexico |
| Dr Rajesh Johnsam | Australia |
| Dr Diane Kalendra | Australia |
| Prof. Vasudha Kamat | India |
| Prof. Nene Ernest Khalema | South Africa |
| Dr Anand Kumar | India |
| Dr Elyssabeth Leigh | Australia |
| Dr Cathryn Lloyd | Australia |

| | |
|---|---|
| Ms Meg Lonergan | Canada |
| Dr David MacLaren | Australia |
| Dr Tome Mapotse | South Africa |
| Dr Jayna McCalman | Australia |
| Dr Janet McIntyre | Australia |
| Dr John Molineux | Australia |
| Adj Ass. Prof Richard Monypenny | Australia |
| Dr Marian Naidoo | UK |
| Ms Margaret O'Connell | Australia |
| Dr Elizabeth Orr | Australia |
| Dr Terry Parminter | New Zealand |
| Dr Paul Pettigrew | UK |
| Dr Eileen Piggot-Irvine | New Zealand |
| Dr Fariza Puteh-Behak | Malaysia |
| Dr Michelle Redman-MacLaren | Australia |
| Ms Riripeti Reedy | New Zealand |
| Prof Wendy Rowe | Canada |
| Dr Akihiro Saito | Japan |
| Prof Shankar Sankaran | Australia |
| Assoc. Prof. Sandro Serpa | Portugal |
| Dr Steve Smith | Australia |
| Dr Anne Stephens | Australia |
| Prof Emmanuel Tetteh | USA |
| Dr Vicki Vaartjes | Australia |
| Dr John Vodonick | USA |
| Prof Jack Whitehead | UK |
| Assoc. Prof. John Wilkinson | Australia |
| Prof Lesley Wood | South Africa |
| Dr Janette Young | Australia |

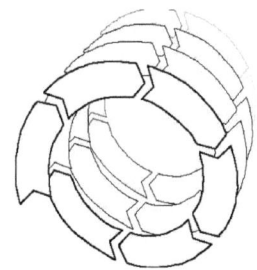

# ALAR Journal

## Volume 26 No 2
## December 2020

ISSN 1326-964X (Print)
ISSN 2206-611X (Online)

### CONTENTS

Editorial     7

Imagine tomorrow: Practitioner learning for the future in Living Educational Theory research     17

    Jack Whitehead

How a case study utilizing action learning and action research enhanced public service excellence on a Federal research campus     45

    Christopher Sigle and Emmanuel Tetteh

An action learning intervention on work-family balance     77

    John Molineux, Rodney Carr and Adam Fraser

| Improving self-learning and dealing with adjustment challenges through individual reflective action research of an international MBA student | 107 |
|---|---|
| Tanya Ahmed | |
| Membership information and article submissions | 132 |

© 2020. Action Learning, Action Research Association Ltd and the author(s) jointly hold the copyright of *ALAR Journal* articles.

# Editorial

I am happy to introduce this important issue for the journal. The impact of Covid-19 has been felt throughout the world this far. Many human activities, including academic and research activities have profusely been affected. I am grateful to the Creator that I am still alive like many may feel, I suppose. However, I would not have uttered these words in this introduction had it not been for the authors who contributed the papers that I am introducing. I am thankful that they are alive, too, and greatly appreciate their patience for the time it took to produce this issue.

Action learning and action research provide the opportunities to reflect on the issues within relational spaces. The papers being introduced, therefore, find relevance in drawing strength even during the dark cloud of Covid-19. In particular, the paper, *Imagine Tomorrow: Practitioner Learning for the Future in Living Educational Theory research* by Whitehead offers explanations from a Living Educational Theory research to Action Research which are focused on the practitioner learning for the future. These two emerge from the educational conversations that accept the point about societal renewal for the future expressed in the citation that Whitehead draws from below:

> Society needs to be renewed by making a shift from the negative energy of fear, competition, control and war to the positive energy of faith, love, hope and creativity. Clearly, we need to conceptualize and practice not just learning conferences but Loving Learning Conferences (Zuber-Skerritt, 2017, p. 224) (p. 17).

Though this paper is not about Covid-19 pandemic, the Living Educational Theory research partly provides its relevance to the situation – the war that humanity faces currently is the ravaging Covid-19. I therefore thought to contextualize the introduction of this paper within Covid-19 in as far as learning that needs to be achieved as purported in the paper. The question is: Do we wait to die or choose to be tenacious and hopeful about life? That is, do we have a belief that the future is still bright for us and that we will make it? This finds truth in Whitehead's description of the living-educational-theory; it

> is an individual's explanation of their educational influence in their own learning, in the learning of others and in the learning of the social formations that influence practice and understandings... Living Educational Theory research refers to the conceptual understandings of the living-educational-theories of individual. In Living Educational Theory research, the individual **generates** their own explanation of their educational influence in learning, rather than deduces it from a previously existing conceptual framework (p. 19, emphasis in original).

The author moves from section one in which he distinguish between a living-educational-theory and Living Educational Theory research, through to section five. He meticulously engages the grammatical symbols and rules to articulate these differences:

> In section five I focus on explanatory principles in explanations of educational influences in learning, in imagining tomorrow, in practitioner learning for the future in Living Educational Theory research. The explanatory principles include relationally dynamic values that are clarified in the course of their emergence in educational conversations. In these conversations individuals, within community, demonstrate that they share an understanding and commitment to live as fully as possible shared values as they project themselves into an imagined future that includes their practitioner-learning in Living Educational Theory research with values that carry hope for human flourishing (p. 21).

Acknowledging the bearing of age (76 years old) on the contribution that is left for him to make still, Whitehead promises to leave a legacy that is expressed in this paper and provides directions to the young researchers to continue the practice of Living Educational Theory research when he is gone. One appreciates the focused contribution that he has lived this far to make in the field. His commitment towards exploring living-educational-theories spans over 1973 to 2000 and now at the University of Bath. It will outlive him and continue to benefit humanity.

According to this author, individuals should "generate their own explanations of their educational influences in their own learning rather than to deduce the explanations from a general conceptual framework of a traditional theory"(p. 23) – the value of action learning and action research. Here, Living Educational Theory research presents an individual with the opportunity to learn in a transformative manner. What the author is trying to say, is that the Living Educational Theory research brings fresh thinking into research – a mindset shift to have research benefit humanity and create hope for the future in a relational space. For example, he argues that "the role that living theories can play and what can be learnt from other cultures who have held them as inseparable from how they express meaning to life. Specifically, he makes reference to the non-Western or indigenous approaches from which a lot can be learnt that traditional research frameworks were divorced from. In the light of the response to Covid-19, for instance, there are learnings that humanity can draw from in terms of clinging to the fundamentals of Ubuntu in relation to social distancing – Africans have found alternative ways of expressing Ubuntu, such as increasing making phone and/or video calls to check on their loved ones and friends, making donations of goods and food to the hungry, etc. Many have reverted to their traditional medicinal practices as preventative measures against the coronavirus, e.g. *Lengana* (Artemisia afra). Myself have gone out to find *lengana* to plant it in my yard.

The author acknowledges the obvious living out Living Educational Theory research which can be witnessed in acting out indigenous knowledge systems by indigenous people.

In the light of the transformative function of Living Educational Theory research, he cites Budd Hall (2015), the Holder of the UNESCO Chair in Community-Based Research and Social

Responsibility in Higher Education, who uses systemic thinking from critical theory and participatory research to generate the following questions for himself:

1. How do I 'decolonize', 'deracialise,' demasculinise and degender my inherited 'intellectual spaces?'

2. How do I support the opening up of spaces for the flowering of epistemologies, ontologies, theories, methodologies, objects and questions other than those that have long been hegemonic, and that have exercised dominance over (perhaps have even suffocated) intellectual and scholarly thought and writing?

3. How do I contribute to the building of new academic cultures and, more widely, new inclusive institutional cultures that genuinely respect and appreciate difference and diversity – whether class, gender, national, linguistic, religious, sexual orientation, epistemological or methodological in nature?

4. How do I become a part of creating the new architecture of knowledge that allows co-construction of knowledge between intellectuals in academia and intellectuals located in community settings? (p. 26)

Whitehead, through the Living Educational Theory research, bridges the gap that exists between academia and communities out there as a way to address a colonial approach to research. He does this by emphasizing a "We" dialogical or conversational relationships. This transitioning emphasizes the values of human flourishing. He thus acknowledges an excerpt from Gumede and Mellet (2019, p. 23 – see this issue, p. 29) about ubuntu; the two authors, endowed immersed in their respective cultures, were committed to let their research make them learn from each other.

This paper, like many others that Whitehead has produced, uses the power of multi-media to represent the ideals of the Living Educational Theory research. A take-home point is that the role that technology can play in research cannot be undermined. Fuelled by the demands of the Fourth Industrial Revolution and restrictions presented by Covid-19, technology has become the research of an international MBA student in Philippines. Ahmed, who comes from Bangladesh, uses self-reflective process and self-reflection methodology to deal with issues of adjustments in an institutional environment in Philippine. She digs into the self-reflection methodology literature such as Dewey (1933) and Hargreaves and Daw (1990) to help her engage in self-reflection. Furthermore, she uses a set of questions by Johns (2004), Coghlan and Brannick (2010) and Schein's ORJI framework of observation, emotional reaction, judgment and intervention. All this helps her to deal with inner self, reflect on her actions, revise her concerns and adjust her personal and social needs.

The author explores the challenges of adjustment in the university environment that she has to acclimatize with which include, but are not limited to, language difficulties, cultural changes and various other hurdles in communication with the staffs and peers. The literature that she explores also adds the fact that international students experience fatigue, anxiety, feelings of alienation, differing social interactions, cultural shock, financial struggles, lack of sufficient accommodation, solitude and loneliness, among others (Bradley, 2000, Erichsen & Bolliger, 2011, Lee & Rice, 2007).

The paper argues that untried methods of interaction in a lecture room setup makes lecturers to be uninformed about academic norms and rules, insufficient support for learning, problems developing interpersonal relationships with local students and lacking a sense of belongingness. A reader may deduce from this argument, that unilinear or mathematical-logical methods which are packaged under "instruction" instead of "facilitation" of learning play a role in failing to promote the accommodation of international students in learning. In the light of the introduction of the first paper in this editorial, the Living Educational Theory research could help remedy this situation. Taking others on board in an academic activity can make them feel at home – this will ensure the achievement of the goal of human flourishing.

Though the paper is a self-reflective paper from an action research point of view, it does not restrict the reader to what an international student can learn only or efforts that the student work can spill over to the home environment and result in conflict" (p. 78).

The authors identify the sources of conflict from the literature which include job stress, excessive job demands and the need to bring work home. The paper hits directly on the experiences that many of us have with the kinds of stress that emanate from the jobs that we do, such as disagreements with line manager, promotional issues, favouritism and so on. When we thought that the computer age brought lightness to the job, the opposite seems to be true – the computer plus internet age has extended the hours of work and is the cause of carry-home work. In meetings, conferences or during travelling, people can be seen answering emails, signing off documents, scheduling meetings, etc. This makes the employee to give priority to the work that needs to be completed at the expense of family. In a complex and technology-depended life and time of today, people yearn for coping strategies to navigate their way between work and family in a more balanced way.

The paper offers light on some strategies that can reduce the negative spillover of conflict which are both extrinsic and intrinsic to the worker. For example, extrinsic strategies can include supervisory and organizational support. The authors keep a focus on intrinsic strategies. The results of their reported study in this paper suggest that, "on average, exposure to the ideas in the workshops led employees to develop a more positive mind-state and improved perception of work-family balance".

The last paper by Ahmed is titled *Improving self-learning and dealing with adjustment challenges through individual reflective action research of an international MBA student*. The WFB issues that the above paper by Molineux, Carr and Fraser raise relate closely with Ahmed's paper. If I were to use the word conflict, I would say that Ahmed's paper addresses an inner conflict that an international student is confronted with having to adjust to the institutional demands and culture. Instead, Ahmed uses the word challenges. The purpose of her paper is improving self-learning and dealing with adjustment challenges through individual reflective action

The authors relied on relevant literature to tackle the identified gap. For example, Frederickson suggests that the public sector leaders must recognize and promote a broader understanding of the concepts pertaining to public life as distinct from for-profit activities while building organizational culture and perspective. Ethical concerns, recognition and reward issues have implications regarding social capital affecting public value. As such, relationship building is essential to program success. Moreover, interpersonal collaboration can be designed into the position itself. Corrupt behaviour, greed and selfishness have proven to compromise the ethics of service provision, playing down human flourishing and undermining the ideals of Ubuntu. The authors engage the PAR framework, Look, Think and Act as well as Schalock's (2001) outcome-based evaluative model to frame a transformative approach to the SSS. The main finding of their research is that more than 67% of those surveyed believed that social capital enhanced SSSP public value. SSSP should therefore be social capital-driven if at all it is to satisfy the public.

The paper, *An action learning intervention on work-family balance* is also interesting as it addresses the problem of work versus family demands with a possible conflict resulting from the imbalance that may ensue. It is interesting in the sense that the reader who is an employee may identify closely with the issues raised in the paper as he/she may be affected by the problem that the authors tackle. The paper explores the impact of an action learning intervention using positive psychological techniques to impact work-family balance (WFB). The authors of this paper, Molineux, Carr and Fraser, define WFB as a concept that fits under the general umbrella of work-life balance, but, as the name implies, is focussed on aspects of the way work and family-life relate to one another. The groups participants in the study were given time to discuss and operationalize their ideas, and then commit to take an appropriate action to their work and family contexts. The subject of work-family balance in this paper raises the issues of work that may cause conflict between work and the family if they are not well controlled. According to the authors, "things that happen at vehicle for human interaction and activities. In the light of the Living Educational Theory research, however, caution needs to be sounded not to advance technologism (perpetuation of colonialism now in the form of technology). Modern technology is mainly a version of colonial culture whereas soft skills are mostly prevalent in indigenous communities, e.g. collectivism, respect, unity. Forging forward with seeking solutions to the human problems, therefore necessitates collaboration between the Western culture and indigenous culture to the extent possible – for human flourishing.

Whitehead's ideas connect well with the second paper, *How a Case Study Utilizing Action Learning and Action Research Enhanced Public Service Excellence on a Federal Research Campus,* by Sigle and Tetteh. These authors examined the ways that the Shared Services Support Program (SSSP) could enhance the primary science mission on a federal research campus through an action learning and action research case study. They identify a gap that public administrators often struggle to lead organizations that are balancing mission requirements with diminishing resources because they are capital-driven rather than social capital-driven. They engage social capital theory to establish a connection between shared services theory and public value theory in the light of the hypothesized influence of social capital on public value.

The authors feel that SSSP managers must be flexible towards change. Indeed, in the current world order when there is a fervent call to be community minded, the SSS must actually act what they profess with "shared" – share ideals and services with communities for human flourishing rather than share profit at the expense of communities. According to the authors, "this includes looking for ways to improve program efficacy by leveraging social capital that impacts public value of service delivery" (p. 52). They back up this claim with Head and Alford (2015), who claims that "adaptive thinking is required for public program managers when they are faced with shifting resources and new strategic directions" (p. 52). Investment in "social capital can influence public value with implications for employee motivation" (p. 53).

must make to adjust. It also has crucial implications about the institutional culture's own self-reflection. This claim finds truth in Ahmed's self-reflective ideas tapering into "the significance of this research for me" and "the significance of this research for us and for them". It all connects to the transitioning of "I" to "We" that is entertained in Whitehead's paper – in an academic environment, how can we accommodate cultural diversity to make the spaces we dominate a home to international students as well? How can we build a community of learning with them?

Prof. Mishack Gumbo
December 2020

# UNIQUE STRATEGIC ALLIANCE

The Global Centre for Work Applied Learning and the Action Learning Action Research Association have established a unique strategic alliance to provide professional development and certification for change leaders in organisations and communities.

GCWAL, an organisational change specialist, uses the Work-Applied Learning (WAL) model which is grounded in Action Research, Action Learning and Reflective Practice. ALARA is a global membership association focussed on the use of Action Learning and Action Research.

As part of the alliance, GCWAL will make available a series of professional development programmes. Upon successful completion, ALARA and GCWAL will co-badge professional certifications such as **Action Learning Facilitators, Action Learning Practitioners and WAL Change Practitioners**. Other certifications will be available as time progresses.

In addition, ALARA will offer complimentary membership to participants in the professional development programmes. ALARA and GCWAL will also undertake collaborative research in the areas of Action Research, Action Learning and Work-Applied Learning.

Further details of the alliance are provided on www.gcwal.com.au and www.alarassociation.org

# Imagine tomorrow: Practitioner learning for the future in Living Educational Theory research

Jack Whitehead

## Abstract

*This paper offers explanations from a Living Educational Theory research approach to Action Research. The explanations are focused on practitioner learning for the future. They emerge from educational conversations that accept the point about societal renewal for the future:*

> *Society needs to be renewed by making a shift from the negative energy of fear, competition, control and war to the positive energy of faith, love, hope and creativity. Clearly, we need to conceptualize and practice not just learning conferences but Loving Learning Conferences (Zuber-Skerritt, 2017, p. 224).*

*Contributions to previous Action Learning and Action Research conferences, that include the Action Research Networks of the Americas (ARNA), the Collaborative Action Research Network (CARN) and the Action Learning Action Research Association (ALARA), are analysed to explain how imagining tomorrow is included in the educational learning of practitioner-researchers who are contributing to the creation of the future, today.*

*The paper is grounded in the practice of individual practitioner-researchers as they generate their own living-educational-theories as explanations of their educational influences in learning, in enquiries of the kind, 'How do I improve what I am doing?' and 'How do we improve what we are doing?'. The explanations include an evaluation of previous learning in making sense of the present together with an imagined possibility of a future that it not yet realized.*

*Meanings of good and educational conversations are clarified and used to demonstrate how authentic 'we' questions can be generated in relation to living as fully as possible values that carry hope for the flourishing of humanity (Gumede & Mellett, 2019). Meanings of participatory, ~i~we~I~us~ relationships (Mounter, 2019) are clarified and used as explanatory principles in explanations of educational influence that are contributing to a global social movement of practitioner-researchers who are contributing to creating a future with hope.*

**Key words:** Living Educational Theory research; educational influences in learning; global social movement

---

**What is known about the topic?**

The originality of the topic is focused on the clarification and use of relationally dynamic values as explanatory principles of educational influences in learning in inquiries of the kind, 'How do I improve what I am doing?

**What does this paper add?**

It adds an understanding of the ways in which AL and AR scholars and practitioners can contribute their living-educational-theories to a global social movement for enhancing the flow of values and understandings that carry hope for human flourishing.

**Who will benefit from its content?**

Practitioner-researchers who wish to both improve their practice and contribute to the knowledge-base of education

**What is the relevance to AL and AR scholars and practitioners?**

It offers a relationally dynamic understanding of the unique constellation of values used by AL and AR scholars and practitioners in improving their practice and generating and sharing their living-educational-theories.

---

*Received   December 2019      Reviewed   July 2020         Published   December 2020*

# Introduction

As I focus on my presentation 'Imagine Tomorrow: Practitioner Learning for the Future in Living Educational Theory research', I don't want to simply repeat ideas from my previous presentations to Collaborative Action Research Network (CARN), Action Research Network of the Americas (ARNA) and Action Learning Action Research Association (ALARA) Conferences and previous publications over the last 50 years of practice as a professional educator and educational researcher. I shall however explain where I am drawing on these previous presentations and publications in imagining tomorrow in practitioner learning to show how Action Research might profitably draw on Living Educational Theory research to contribute to a future with values of human flourishing.

To fulfil the aim of imagining tomorrow in practitioner learning for the future in Living Educational Theory research, the paper is organized into five sections: clarifying a distinction between a living-educational-theory and Living Educational Theory research; meanings of good and educational conversations (Gadamer, 1975; Mellett, 2020); meanings of ~i~we~I~us~ relationships; generating, researching and answering authentic 'we' questions; explanatory principles in explanations of educational influences in learning in contributing to the creation of a future.

In section one I distinguish between a living-educational-theory and Living Educational Theory research, using lower case, hyphens and capitals to clarify the difference. A living-educational-theory is an individual's explanation of their educational influence in their own learning, in the learning of others and in the learning of the social formations that influence practice and understandings. Living Educational Theory research refers to the conceptual understandings of the living-educational-theories of individual. The distinction is important because in Living Educational Theory research it is not possible, as it is in traditional theorizing, to **deduce** an explanation of an individual's educational influence from the general conceptual framework of the theory. In Living Educational Theory research, the individual **generates** their own explanation of their educational influence in learning, rather than deduces it from a previously existing conceptual framework. These explanations draw on insights from a wide range of ways of knowing, including, intuitive, experiential, presentations, conceptual and dialectical in forming a living-educational-theory of educational influences in practice. Because of the importance in this paper of the meaning of what is educational and of distinguishing learning from what is educational, these meanings will be clarified.

In section two I focus on meanings of good and educational conversations from Gadamer (1975) and Mellett (2020). Continuing the focus in section one on what is educational, I focus on the explanations of educational influences in learning that are emerging from good and educational conversations. I clarify the meanings of an educational conversation in terms of learning with values of human flourishing (Reiss & White, 2013). Referring back to a paper in Teaching Today for Tomorrow (Whitehead, 2003), I highlight the importance of digital visual data in clarifying meanings of the expression of embodied values that carry hope from human flourishing. I refer to digital visual data from the editorial board of the Educational Journal of Living Theories and to the post-doctoral Living Educational Theory research group to relate good and educational conversations to Living Educational Theory research as a social movement that are extending the influences of Living Educational Theory research with values that carry hope for human flourishing.

In section three I focus on meanings of participatory, ~i~we~I~us~ relationships (Mounter, 2019; Mounter et al., 2019) with their use of the ~ symbol. As I was walking to the stage with my interpreter to present a keynote to the 6th Japan Academy of Diabetes Education in Osaka (Whitehead, 2001) I received a shock when the interpreter asked which of the 16 meanings of 'I' should he focus on in his interpretation. You might imagine my shock as I had taken for granted that my meaning of 'I' in my question, 'How do I improve what I am doing?' was unproblematic! Hence, my awareness of the importance of clarifying the meanings of the words I use to communicate the nature of educational relationships in Living Educational Theory research. I do not believe that this clarification is an easy task. In my early research between 1970 to 1990 I used Martin Buber's (1958) insights in his poetic work 'I and Thou' to communicate the quality of I-You relationships in my educational relationships.

As my research focus evolved from a focus on explaining my educational influences in my own learning and in the learning of others, to explaining my educational influences in the learning of social formations, I have recognized the importance of working and researching within communities of Living Educational Theory researchers. This is because the influences of many individuals are needed to develop a global influence in the educational learning of social formations. I acknowledged above the influence of Alan Rayner's understanding of natural inclusion in the evolution of my own relationally dynamic awareness of space and boundaries. In section three I acknowledge the influence of Alan Rayner's ideas of natural inclusion in the evolution of complex communities, together with Joy Mounter's understandings of ~i~we~I~us~ relationships in explanation the educational influences of an individual in the learning of a social formations with values that carry hope for human flourishing. I am thinking of the values that Briganti (2020) uses in her thesis on 'My living-educational-theory of International Development'. These are the relationally dynamic values of empathy, social and gender justice, outrage, responsibility, love for and faith in humanity and dignity. I draw attention to these values and the questions that are of significance to the flourishing of human community in the Interim Conclusion below.

In section four I focus on generating, researching and answering authentic 'we' questions. I believe that all readers will recognize a tension between someone using 'we' in a way that seeks to include you in the 'we' and that you feel a resistance to your 'I' being included the 'we'. At other times I imagine that you agree with 'we' statements or questions such as, 'How do we improve what we are doing?'

In section five I focus on explanatory principles in explanations of educational influences in learning, in imagining tomorrow, in practitioner learning for the future in Living Educational Theory research. The explanatory principles include relationally dynamic values that are clarified in the course of their emergence in educational conversations. In these conversations individuals, within community, demonstrate that they share an understanding and commitment to live as fully as possible shared values as they project themselves into an imagined future that includes their practitioner-learning in Living Educational Theory research with values that carry hope for human flourishing. These values are the ethical principles used by Living Educational Theory researchers to evaluate their attempts to improve their practice and to live their values as fully as possible.

As a 76 year old, I recognize that the contribution I can make to the future, in my lifetime, is limited. Hence, in the interim conclusion I focus on the contributions young practitioner learners are making to imagining tomorrow in their living-educational-theories with values of human flourishing.

## Clarifying a distinction between a living-educational-theory and Living Educational Theory research

I put forward the idea that individual practitioner-researchers could generate their own living-educational-theories as explanations of their educational influences in their own learning, in the learning of others and in the learning of social formations (Whitehead, 1985, 1989, 2018), as a response to an error in the then dominant disciplines approach to educational theory. The disciplines approach to educational theory held that educational theory was constituted by the disciplines of the philosophy, psychology, sociology and history of education. It also held that the practical principles I used to explain my educational influences in my own learning were at best pragmatic maxims that had a first crude and superficial justification in practice that in any rationally developed theory would be replaced by principles with more fundamental theoretical justification. My definition of a 'living' educational theory emerged from Ilyenkov's (1977, p. 313) question, 'If an object exists as a living contradiction, what must the thought be that expresses it?' I experienced my 'I' as a living contradiction as I explored the implications of asking, researching and answering my question, 'How do I improve what I am doing in my professional practice?' I held the view that a professional would be contributing to their professional knowledge-base. I say my own contribution in terms of generating and making public my explanation of my educational influences in learning.

In my work and educational research at the University of Bath between 1973-2000, my primary focus was on the academic legitimating of the living-educational-theories of individuals. With the successful legitimation of these theories, other researchers suggested that the time was right to develop a conceptual understanding of Living Educational Theory research as a research approach or paradigm. This led to the development in 2008 of the Educational Journal of Living Theories (https://ejolts.net).

I still feel a tension between meanings of a living-educational-theory and Living Educational Theory research because of traditional meanings of theory. In tradition theories an explanation of an individual's practice would be derived from the general conceptual framework of the theory. The conceptual framework of Living Educational Theory research allows individuals to place their research within a research community without deducing an explanation of their educational influences in learning from the concept framework of Living Educational Theory research. It is for individual practices to generate their own explanations of their educational influences in their own learning rather than to deduce the explanations from a general conceptual framework of a traditional theory. I hope my distinction between generating and deducing is clear.

In gaining academic legitimacy for living-educational-theories, I bear in mind Patti Lather's point about ironic validity, highlighted by Donmoyer (1996):

> Contrary to dominant validity practices where the rhetorical nature of scientific claims is masked with methodological assurances, a strategy of ironic validity proliferates forms, recognizing that they are rhetorical and without foundation, post epistemic, lacking in epistemological support. The text is resituated as a representation of its 'failure to represent what it points toward but can never reach....' (Lather, 1994, p. 40-41).

This recognition of never reaching, in our representations our educational influences in learning, the educational influences themselves, continues to motivate me to find forms of representation that get as close as possible to the educational influences themselves.

During 2002, I became familiar with Rayner's (2004) understanding of natural inclusion as an awareness of space and boundaries as connective, reflexive and co-created. Here is a video of Rayner's communication that transformed my epistemology from a dialectical epistemology that held insights from propositional theories, to an inclusional epistemology (Whitehead & Rayner, 2006) that held insights from dialectical and propositional theories: https://www.youtube.com/watch?v=yVa7FUIA3W8

Whilst I now use digital visual data, to communicate meanings of the embodied expressions of the meanings of my values, I am not expecting you to view all the video clips. You could however access the analysis of the limitations of text-based communications, relative to multimedia texts presented to the seventh World Congress of Action Learning Action Research and Process Management and Participatory Action Research (Whitehead & Huxtable, 2006a; 2006b).

With this insight, of relationally dynamic awareness, I increased my use of digital visual data in analyses of educational influences in learning. For example, in 2002, I video-recorded supervision sessions with Jacqueline Delong as Jacqueline prepared for the submission of her doctoral thesis. As I move the cursor backwards and forwards along the following clip I shall pause at 43-46 seconds, as moments of empathetic resonance, to communicate our shared meanings of an embodied flow of life-affirming energy that we use as an explanatory principle in explanations of our educational influences in learning: https://www.youtube.com/watch?reload=9&v=w2kdOfRKFYs. A more detailed analysis of this work was presented at the 2016 CARN conference (Whitehead, 2016).

The present focus of my research on imagining tomorrow in practitioner learning for the future in Living Educational Theory research is on explaining the educational influences in the learning of social formations. Because of this interest in influencing the learning social formations, I am focusing on the living-educational-theories of practitioners that are emerging from communities of Living Educational Theory researchers who are seeking to enhance the flow of values and explanations that carry hope for human flourishing. In the generation of explanations that get as close as possible to the educational influences themselves, I am again influenced by Rayner's ideas. At this point of my research, I am influenced by his ideas (Rayner, 2019) on the naturally inclusive evolution of complex communities with receptive-responsive relationships.

In our receptive-responsive relationships with each other, our Living Educational Theory research communities and our contexts, we are expressing our life-affirming energies and explanations of educational influences in learning, with values that carry hope for human flourishing. We are evolving our individual and collective identities in strengthening our resilience and responsiveness to changing circumstances as we seek to enhance the flow of values and living-educational-theories that are contributing to human flourishing. We also recognize and seek to understand and transcend those influences that are hindering the development and extensions of our Living Educational Theory community as a social movement.

Some of these influences focus on culturally distinctive approaches to action research and action learning, especially in relation to non-Western/indigenous approaches to educational research. Masters and Whitehead (2017) have related action research to the narratives of indigenous people who may wish to further improve practice or deepen their understandings with Living Theories and vice-versa. Henry (1991) at the First World Conference of Action Learning, Action Research and Process Management criticized many of the contributions for not being clear about the principles they were using to distinguish their Action Learning and Action

Research. At the Second World Conference I explained (Whitehead, 1992) how my philosophy of action research had transformed and improved my professional practice and contributed to the production of a good social order:

> The purpose of this paper is to draw attention to a new form of educational theory for improving professional practice and producing a good social order. The recent literature on action learning and action research has focused on their appropriateness as methods to develop managerial and other professional competences. Theoretical frameworks of action research have emphasised conceptual rather than dialectical forms of knowledge. This paper questions the emphasis on method and conceptual theories and argues for a greater concentration on the creation and testing of a living and dialectical educational theory for professional practice within which one's own philosophy of education in engaged as a first-person participant (p. 436).

In relation to research on systemic thinking and practices, Living Educational Theory researchers engage with insights from these researchers. For example, Hall (2015), the co-Holder of the UNESCO Chair in Community-Based Research and Social Responsibility in Higher Education, has used systemic thinking from critical theory and participatory research to generate the following questions for himself:

1. How do I 'decolonize', 'deracialise,' demasculinise and degender my inherited 'intellectual spaces?'

2. How do I support the opening up of spaces for the flowering of epistemologies, ontologies, theories, methodologies, objects and questions other than those that have long been hegemonic, and that have exercised dominance over (perhaps have even suffocated) intellectual and scholarly thought and writing?

3. How do I contribute to the building of new academic cultures and, more widely, new inclusive institutional cultures that genuinely respect and appreciate difference and diversity – whether class, gender, national, linguistic, religious, sexual orientation, epistemological or methodological in nature?

4. How do I become a part of creating the new architecture of knowledge that allows co-construction of knowledge between intellectuals in academia and intellectuals located in community settings? (Hall, 2015, p. 12)

These questions emphasise the importance of systemic thinking in generating questions that focus on improving systems. In a recent analysis of moving from Action Research to Activism with Living Educational Theory research, I (Whitehead, 2020) have emphasised that such questions are a necessary component of engaging with issues of enhancing a social formation, but they are not sufficient. It is important to explore the implications of asking such questions in one's own practice:

> In terms of research and action aims I want to emphasise the necessity of including 'I' with such questions. Asking such 'I' question is a necessary but not sufficient condition in contributing to moving action research to activism with Living Educational Theory research. Having fulfilled the necessary but not sufficient condition of asking such 'I' questions it is sufficient to fulfil one's educational responsibility of practically exploring the implications of asking, researching and answering such questions, as an activist. This responsibility is explored below in methodology, theoretical tools and methods (p. 60).

Before I focus on the generation of 'we' questions and claims, I want to consider meanings of good and educational conversations because explanations of educational influences in learning within communities of practitioners are grounded in dialogical or conversational relationships.

## Meanings of good and educational conversations

I identify a good conversation with what Gadamer (1975, p. 367) refers to as the art of conversation. Gadamer says that to conduct a dialogue requires first of all that the partners do not talk at cross purposes. Hence it necessarily has the structure of question and answer. Gadamer points out that the first condition of the art of conversation is ensuring that the other person is with us. He says that to conduct a conversation means to allow oneself to be conducted by the subject matter to which the partners in the dialogue are oriented. It requires that one does not try to argue the other person down but that one really considers the weight of the other's opinion.

For Gadamer, a conversation involves the art of testing and he stresses that the art of testing is the art of questioning. He emphasises that questioning makes the object and all the possibilities fluid and is thus against the fixity of opinions. Hence, a person skilled in the 'art' of questioning is a person who can prevent questions being suppressed by the dominant opinion. A person who possesses this art will himself search for everything in favour of an opinion. For Gadamer, conversations do not consist of trying to discover the weakness of what is said, but in bringing out its real strength. Conversation is not the art of arguing, which he says can make a strong case out of a weak one, but in the art of thinking which can strengthen objections by referring to the subject matter.

These are the qualities that I am claiming constitute a good conversation and that I include in my understanding of an educational conversation. What I add to a good conversation, to distinguish it as an educational conversation, is learning with values that carry hope for human flourishing. I am stressing the values of human flourishing, in practitioner learning in creating the future, because not all learning is educational. Being born in 1944 when millions of individuals were being killed in extermination camps, I know that history is full of examples of individuals, communities and societies where learning has violated the values that contribute to the flourishing of humanity.

In imagining tomorrow with practitioner learning for the future in Living Educational Theory research I shall now focus on the generation of 'we' questions in educational conversations. I see 'we' questions as involving shared values within Living Educational Theory communities that are exploring the implications of asking, researching and answering 'we' questions of the kind, 'How do we improve what we are doing in extending and deepening the influence of Living Educational Theory research as a social movement with values that carry hope for human flourishing?'

## Generating, researching and answering authentic 'we' questions in educational conversations

Working and researching within Living Educational Theory communities involves learning from each other. For example, Gumede and Mellett (2019) have explained how they have generated, researched and answered 'we' questions in their educational conversations on "Forming a 'we' through good quality conversations".

> Many Living Educational Theory papers are jointly authored and written with a voice that uses the collective pronoun 'We'. By what process can separate, isolated 'I's claim to become a composite 'We'? This paper discusses the process by which its authors – two initially separate authoring voices – came to feel able to claim that they can speak as a believable and authentic 'We'. The process of that merging develops around the concept of a 'good quality conversation'. The authors come from two radically different cultural traditions which they describe as the 'oralate' culture of South Africa that predominated before the spread of 19th century colonialism and the 'literate' culture of Western Europe that developed from the 17th century Enlightenment. Starting with the production of intersecting autobiographical accounts, they form their 'We' by progressively helping each other to 'get on the inside' of each other's culture. In Living Educational Theory terms, this is the process of each author's educational influence on the other. Engaging with de Santos' (1997) ideas of intercultural translation and with Jousse (1997), they seek "…discoveries [that] consist in the bringing together of ideas susceptible to being connected, which have hitherto been isolated" (p. 49) to create a shared form of knowledge." Coming together to speak as 'We' also involves the identification of shared values and their expression in each of the author's separate lived contexts. These shared values lead them to identify a commonality within the tenets of Ubuntu – a person is a person through

other persons – on which they base questions that have relevance for the future flourishing of Humanity (Gumede & Mellett, 2019, p. 23).

Mellett is leading the way and, along with Laidlaw and Cunningham, is showing how educational conversations and 'we' enquiries can be supported by social media, such as the wiki technology. For example, if you click on the following links you can access Mellett's responses to questions of the kind, 'What use has all this effort been, in terms of the influence of the Editorial Board of the Educational Journal of Living Theories (EJOLTS) community:

http://ejolts-wiki.mattrink.co.uk/index.php/Main_Page

http://ejolts-wiki.mattrink.co.uk/index.php/Pete

http://ejolts-wiki.mattrink.co.uk/index.php/Pete%27s_Question

Cunningham is a prison visitor in the Republic of Ireland. He visits prisoners who have been found guilty of the most serious of crimes. Educational conversations between Cunningham and Laidlaw challenge me to recognize and relate to the values of human flourishing within those who have committed such crimes. The educational conversations seem to me to offer a different grounding to a criminal justice and rehabilitation service to the ones that presently dominate both the UK and the Republic of Ireland.

You can access the educational conversations between Moira Laidlaw and Ben Cunningham. The following link gives you access to what for me is the most challenging of their educational conversations, as practitioner-researchers, about the values they are seeking to live as fully as possible in contributing to the flourishing of humanity:

http://ejolts-wiki.mattrink.co.uk/index.php/Ben

The following link gives you access to Laidlaw's responses to Mellett's question about 'What use has all this effort been?' in relation to the influences of the EJOLTS community:

http://ejolts-wiki.mattrink.co.uk/index.php/Moira

As I continue to focus on the importance of educational conversations in enhancing Practitioner Learning for the Future in Living Educational Theory research, I need to clarify the nature of the relationships in such conversations. In doing this, I have been learning from Joy Mounter, a participant in Living Educational Theory research communities, about the meanings of ~i~we~I~us~ relationships.

## Meanings of ~i~we~I~us~ relationships

Here is Mounter's clarification of meanings of ~i~we~I~us~ relationships that I use in section five in defining explanatory principles in explanations of educational influences in learning of communities of Living Educational Theory researchers:

> '~i~we~I~us~ in Community' as a Definition of Educational Research
>
> My definition of research-led educational professional development takes both aspects from Whitehead (2008) and Huxtable (2016) but I incorporate ' ~i~we~I~us~ in community'. '~i~we~I~us~ in community' defines the flow of energy and developing metacognitive relationships. The understanding of self in relation to others, caring and adding to something bigger than yourself, the desire to make a difference in the world. This addresses the limitation I identified earlier in my understanding of Whitehead's looking at the educational influences in the social formations we are part of. Whether by developing research skills, practice, clarity of embodied values, living-contradictions, combining the movement and flow of energy between the given self (curriculum, professional practice skills and knowledge, teaching standards, targets) and the living self (values, beliefs, passions, strengths, self, actions, place in and of the world). This leads to personal growth and transformation and community growth and transformation.

The tilde ~ represents the ebb and flow of energy, conversational learning and challenge, questioning and validation at differing points. This is the flow of energy that leads to reflection, agency and metacognition. The tilde is before and after the sentence to show this energy and community being part of something bigger than self or the group, but being knowledge creators, offering as a gift to make a difference. The lower case i, is offered by Huxtable and Whitehead (2015, p. 10) as the relational ~i~ in community. This space we represent as i, is also the space of reflection and learning about self, what matters to me, who am I? What do I want my place in the world to be? The upper case I, is the self we offer the world, the self I am, the embodied values I demonstrate, the talents I share, the opinions I voice, the ethics I live by. ~i~we~ shows how the developing 'I' of each person is in community together voiced as 'we.' The inward view of the community. ~i~we~I~ You see the collective of we, the flow of energy within the community of each individual i , offering, questioning, challenging, growing in self and helping others to grow and transform too. The learning and metacognition through that flow of ~i~we~I~ is then seen by others and understanding of self we offer the world as 'I.' ~us~ is vitally important and is the sense of community we have, the selves we offer beyond our community to add to the flourishing of humanity (Whitehead, 2018 ), Frankl's "spark in life", our offer of joining our growth and transformation (Mounter, 2019, pp. 8-9).

## Explanatory principles in explanations of educational influences in learning in contributing to the creation of a future.

In 2003, in a contribution to Teaching Today for Tomorrow (Whitehead, 2003) on 'Creating Our Living Educational Theories in Teaching and Learning to Care: Using Multi-Media to Communicate the Meanings and Influence of our Embodied Educational Values', I suggested that loving care could become an explanatory principle and standard of judgement in the generation and testing of an individual's living-educational-theory. I suggested that readers of Teaching Today for Tomorrow might like to engage in a co-enquiry to see if we can develop some shared understandings of how we are living this value in our educational relationships. I explained that I was thinking of how the educational relationships in which we participate influence the learning of others and educate the social formations in which we live and work.

The idea that you could be having an influence in the education of social formations may not be one at the forefront of your thinking. Its importance to me, as I wrote the 2003 paper, was highlighted by the recent invasion of Iraq by US and UK forces with the subsequent deaths of thousands of Iraqis and hundreds of coalition forces. The fact that social formations are still engaged in warfare in different countries around the world, such as the Yemen and Syria, continues to tell me that there is something wrong with the education of our social formations. Hence, my emphasis on the educational influence of loving care. I pointed out in the 2003 paper that a world organized through such a principle would, it seems to me, be less likely to engage in such destructive activity than our present social orders. So, I continue to stress the importance of bringing loving care more fully into the world as an educational standard that can influence both the lives of individuals and the learning of social formations.

My 2003 paper was an attempt to develop a co-enquiry with readers of 'Teaching Today for Tomorrow. I suggested that in order to develop a shared understanding of what we mean by loving care in our educational relationships, then we will need to show each other what we are doing in these relationships (Fletcher & Whitehead, 2003; Delong & Whitehead, 1998). While most of my research publications up to 2003 had been in the form of journal articles of the kind published in Teaching Today for Tomorrow, I acknowledged the need to develop multi-media forms of representation for accounts of my educational influence with my students and within the social formations where I live and work. In clarifying my explanatory principles in explanations of educational influences in learning in communities of Living Educational

Theory researchers I am emphasizing the importance of multi-media forms of representation.

In referring to the ideas of Deleuze and Guattari below, I want to avoid what Bassey (1991) refers to as three of the traditional academic games of 'genuflecting', 'sandbagging', and 'kingmaking' that he argues should be dropped from academic discourse.

In demonstrating my use of ~i~we~I~us~ relationships in educational community as explanatory principles, I recognise the validity of Deleuze and Guattari's (1994, pp. 5-6) point that concepts, such as the ones I am using as explanatory principles are not waiting for us ready-made, like heavenly bodies. They must be created. For Deleuze (2001) and I agree, a life is made up of virtualities, events, singularities. In imagining tomorrow with practitioner learning for the future in Living Educational Theory research, I am creating a virtual world in the sense of imagined possibilities that are not yet realized in practice, but which I am projecting myself into.

One of these possibilities follows the successful proposal with Swaroop Rawal, Marie Huxtable and Jacqueline Delong for an interactive symposium in the CARN/ALARA Conference of 17-19 October 2019 on 'Imagining tomorrow in the generation of living-educational-theories with learning for the future.' In our overall aims of the session we say that we will show how educational conversations, grounded in values that carry hope for the flourishing of humanity, can contribute to hopeful and loving rocesses of social transformation with these values. We say that ᴧ will show how we are using digital visual data from multi- ᴧen Skype conversations, as conferences as sites of learning and ᴧlopment, and digital technologies in living-posters and a ᴧ Educational Theory Wiki. We say that we will demonstrate ᴧe are using these technologies to sustain and evolve our ducational conversations as we deepen and extend the ᴧnal influences of our practitioner learning for the future in ng to Living Educational Theory research as a social

On the 8th October 2019 we engage in a SKYPE conversation that includes responses to our proposed individual contributions to the symposium. Responses to my contribution include a clarification of meanings of ~i~we~I~us~ relationships (Mounter, 2019) and the use of these relationships as explanatory principles in explanations of educational influence in learning that are emerging from communities of Living Educational Theory researchers as contributions to a global social movement of practitioner-researchers who are creating a future with values that carry hope for human flourishing.

Our responses to Swaroop Rawal's contribution are focused on the long struggle Swaroop experienced while contributing to drafting the life- skills educational policy for the Ministry of Human Resource and Development, India. The responses include a clarification of what Swaroop means by a counter-narrative in her belief that I in this increasingly multicultural world, counter-narratives are an essential and a necessary element of today's narratives as we need to hear the points of view of communities typically ignored or marginalized.

Our responses to Marie Huxtable's contribution are focused on her claim that Living Educational Theory research accounts are contributing to the growth of a professional educational knowledge-base for the flourishing of humanity. Our responses include a focus on the claim that digital, visual data of practice are being used to clarify and communicate, life-affirming ontological and relational values that give professional practice meaning and purpose and are being used in Living Educational Theory research as explanatory principles of educational influence.

Our responses to Jacqueline Delong's contribution are focused on her meanings of creating living-educational-theories in living cultures of inquiry. Our responses focus on the use of digital visual data in developing appropriate forms of representation in dialogic educational research that includes building respectful, democratic, caring and loving relationships in a living culture of inquiry with living-educational-theories that are contributing to practitioner learning for the future.

The video-recording of our responses are analysed using explanatory principles of ~i~we~I~us~ relationships in explanations of educational influences in learning that are emerging from communities of Living Educational Theory researchers. The analysis demonstrates how these communities are contributing to Living Educational Theory research as a social movement with values and understandings that carry hope for human flourishing.

## Interim conclusion

In this paper, on imagining tomorrow with practitioner learning for the future in Living Educational Theory research, I have built on my previous research before moving into new insights into the meanings of ~i~we~I~us~ relationships as explanatory principles in Living Educational Theory research. The new insights are focused on the nature of explanations emerging from within communities of Living Educational Theory researchers that are generating living-educational-theories as explanations for educational influences in the learning of social formations with values that carry hope for the flourishing of humanity. I continue to emphasize the importance of including digital visual data as evidence in explanations of educational influences in learning whilst developing new meanings of relationally dynamic explanatory principles. I have shown how these explanatory principles can be used in imagining tomorrow with practitioner learning for the future in Living Educational Theory research.

In 2019 I was asked by the Editorial Board of the EJOLTS to submit a paper that focused on my 30 years engagement with Living Educational Theory research since my most referenced paper was published (Whitehead, 1989). EJOLTS has now published my paper (Whitehead, 2019). The abstract states:

> 30 years ago, in 1989, a paper of mine was published that is most often referenced in relation to my work in Living Educational Theory research (Whitehead, 1989) I do hope that you will browse through this paper, as an easy introduction, to my ideas about living-educational-theory.

In this 2019 issue of the Educational Journal of Living Theories (EJOLTS), I re-visit the paper in order to share my present understanding of Living Educational Theory research with the help of the EJOLTS open review process. What I have also done, using the hypertext facility enabled by EJOLTS, is to update the six headings of the 1989 paper with my 2019 insights. Another use of technology is the inclusion of digital visual data from educational practices and educational relationships. I clarify and communicate the meanings of the embodied and ontological values that I use as explanatory principles in explanations of educational influences in my own learning, in the learning of others and in the learning of the social formations that influence my practice and understandings.

In 2019, I can provide the evidence from universities around the world that explanations of educational influences in learning have received academic accreditation (https://www.actionresearch.net/living/living.shtml). Having satisfied myself that the validity for this claim is beyond reasonable doubt, I am now focusing on enhancing the influence of Living Educational Theory research as a global social movement with values of human flourishing. I then look forward to the next 30 years to 2049.

In looking forward 30 years on 'Imagine Tomorrow: Practitioner Learning for the Future in Living Educational Theory research', I shall only be present in some of your memories and perhaps in your use of any of my ideas that you are integrating within your own life. In this interim conclusion I want to stress the importance of others who are working and researching together to enhance the educational influences of Living Educational Theory research in a global social movement. Here are two examples from individuals who are young enough to be able to look back in 30 years' time in 2049 on their own productive lives:

On the 9th December 2019 I was present, at the University of Cumbria, as a non-participant observer, at Arianna Briganti's (2020) doctoral viva on the thesis on her living-educational-theory of international development. Here is an extract from her Abstract:

My living-educational-theory of International Development is presented as an original contribution to knowledge. The originality is focused on the relationally dynamic values of empathy, social and gender justice, outrage, responsibility, love for and faith in humanity and dignity. The originality is the use of these values as explanatory principles in my explanation of my educational influences in my own learning, in the learning of others and in the learning of the social formations that influence my practice and understandings.

I was impressed with the way Briganti responded to examiners' questions from within the integrity of herself and her thesis. Briganti is young enough to be able to look forward to another 30 years of contributions to spreading the influence of Living Educational Theory research in International Development. It is such commitments that carry the hope, for me, that Living Educational Theory research and the living-educational-theories of individuals will deepen and extend their influences in human flourishing.

In this paper on 'Imagine Tomorrow: Practitioner Learning for the Future in Living Educational Theory research', I am finishing with the words of Carozzi (2019). Carozzi is the youngest Living Educational Theory researcher. For the future to be influenced by Living Educational Theory research, it will rest on productive lives of such researchers to generate this future. Carozzi states, in her self-enquiry on 'Towards the development of my living-educational-theory research':

> This article is intended as an account of my educational journey that led me from being a passive learner to become the researcher of my own learning processes. I explore two of my relationally-dynamic values (Laidlaw, 2018a) for which I wish my work to be held accountable: hope and responsibility. By looking back at the three years spent studying for the M.Sc. in Development Management (DM) and the few months that followed the submission of my dissertation, I disclose the difficulties, the struggles and the joys of slowly becoming the subject of my own enquiry. The interaction I have with DM as a discipline slowly shifts from

being a passive relationship to becoming a living ontological dimension in my enquiry. This leads me to recognise and appreciate the importance of the aesthetic stance in my encounter with inspirational reads. Moving from the growing emergence of ontological questions, a developing sense of being a living contradiction, and the engagement with the aesthetic dimensions of my own reading experience, I present the subsequent stage of my research: the writing of my Ph.D. proposal in Living Educational Theory research. In it, I stress the necessity to start my research from a self-enquiry, intended as the search for and understanding of my own 'I'. I see the values of hope and responsibility as central in the development of my self-enquiry, which is contributing to the development of my own living-educational-theory research. This offers me the opportunity to consider values as explanatory principles in the explanation of the meanings of my actions; it also requires me to engage in a central Living Educational Theory research question "how can I improve my practice?" which I have found to be linked with issues regarding self-individualization and self-definition (Jung, 1962) (Carozzi 2019, p. 36).

As the world suffers from the coronavirus pandemic we know that our futures will be influenced by what we do and the values of human flourishing that we decide to live by. I have made a case for the importance of generating and sharing our living-educational-theories as action learners and action researchers as we contribute to imagining tomorrow through our practitioner learning in creating the future. As the heart of the case is the recognition of the importance of our relationships and with living as fully as possible the relationally dynamic values that are focused on creating a better world with these values of human flourishing.

# References

Bassey, M. (1991). Creating Education through Research. *British Educational Research Journal*, 18(1), pp. 3-16. Presidential Address to the British Educational Research Association, 29th September 1991 in Nottingham. Retrieved from http://www.bera.ac.uk/files/presidentialaddresses/Bassey,_1991.pdf

Briganti, A. (2020). '*My living-educational-theory of International Development*' PhD Thesis, University of Lancaster. Retrieved from https://www.actionresearch.net/living/ABrigantiphd.pdf

Buber, M. (1958). *I and Thou*. London: T & T Clark.

Carozzi, G. (2019). A self-enquiry: Towards the development of my living-educational-theory research. *Educational Journal of Living Theories*, 12(2), pp. 36-64. Retrieved from https://ejolts.net/node/348

Deleuze, G. (2001). *Pure Immanence: Essays on A Life, with an introduction by John Rajchman*, Translated by Anne Boyman, New York: Zone books.

Deleuze, G. & Guattari, F. (1994). *What is Philosophy?* London: Verso.

Delong, J. & Whitehead, J. (1998). *Continuously regenerating developmental standards of practice in teacher education*. Paper presented at the Ontario Educational Research Council 40th Annual Conference, Toronto, December 4, 1998.

Donmoyer, R. (1996). Educational Research in an Era of Paradigm Proliferation: What's a Journal Editor to Do? *Educational Researcher*, 25(2), pp. 19-25.

Fletcher, S. & Whitehead, J (2003). The 'Look' of the teacher: Using DV to improve the professional practice of teaching in Clarke, A. & Erickson, G. (2003) *Teacher Inquiry: Living the research in everyday practice*. London: Routledge Falmer.

Gadamer, H. G. (1975). *Truth and Method*, London: Sheed and Ward.

Gumede, J. & Mellett, P. (2019). Forming a 'We' through a good quality conversation. *Educational Journal of Living Theories*, 12(1), pp. 23-61.

Hall, B. (2015). *Beyond Epistemicide: Knowledge Democracy and Higher Education*. First presented at the International Symposium on Higher Education in the Age of Neo Liberalism and Audit Cultures, July 21-25, University of Regina 2015. Retrieved from http://unescochair-cbrsr.org/unesco/wpcontent/uploads/2015/09/Beyond_Epistemicide_final.pdf

Henry, C. (1991). If Action Research were Tennis, in Zuber-Skerritt (1991) *Action Learning For Improved Performance. Key contributions to the First World Congress on Action Research and Process Management*. Brisbane, AEBIS Publishing.

Huxtable, M. (2016). Integrating personal, political, and professional educational practice that gives meaning and purpose to my life and work. *Educational Journal of Living Theories*, 9(2), pp. 1-23.

Huxtable, M. & Whitehead, J. (2015). *A Workshop On Living Educational Theory Research: Innovative Research Methods In Researching One's Own Higher Education*. University of Cumbria, Carlisle, 3rd June 2015.

Ilyenkov, E. (1977). *Dialectical Logic*. Moscow: Progress Publishers.

Jung C. G. (1962). *Collected works of C. G. Vol. 7: Two Essays in Analytical Psychology*. 2nd ed. New York: Princeton University Press.

Laidlaw, M. (2018). Living Hope and Creativity as Educational Standards of Judgment. *Educational Journal of Living Theories*, 11(2), pp. 27-64. Retrieved from: https://ejolts.net/node/326

Lather, P. (1994). Fertile obsession: Validity after poststructuralism, in Gitlin, A. (Ed.), Power and method: *Political activism and educational research* (pp. 36-60). London, UK: Routledge.

Masters, K. & Whitehead, J. (2017). A review of Cairns, H. & Harney, I, B. (2014) Four Circles – Customs that are Law in an Aboriginal Cosmoscape: Justice, Mercy and Survival, in Bill Harney's Imulun Wardaman Aboriginal Spiritual Law. (A Northern Australian People with their Intellectual World of Law in the Four Circles Tradition.) Published by Alan Mogridge of Excell Printing Group, Merimbula; Australia. *Educational Journal of Living Theories*, 10(1), pp. 114-124. Retrieved from https://ejolts.net/node/301

Mellett, P. (2020). *Educational Conversations*. Retrieved from http://www.actionresearch.net/writings/mellett/mellettconversation01-10-20.pdf

Mounter, J. (2019). *~i~we~I~us~ relationships*. Retrieved from http://www.spanglefish.com/allicanbe/index.asp?pageid=698540

Mounter, J., Huxtable, M. & Whitehead, J. (2019). Using Thinking Actively in a Social Context and Spirals in Living Educational Theory research in explanations of educational influences in a global social movement. *Gifted Education International*. 35(2), pp. 91-109.

Rayner, A. (2004). Inclusionality and the role of place, space and dynamic boundaries in evolutionary processes. *Philosophica* 73, pp. 51-70.

Rayner, A. (2019). *The naturally inclusive evolution of complex communities*. Personal email communication 23 September 2019.

Reiss, M. J. & White, J. (2013). *An Aims-based Curriculum: The significance of human flourishing for schools*. London: Institute of Education Press.

Whitehead, J. (1985). An analysis of an individual's educational development - the basis for personally orientated action research, in Shipman, M. (Ed.) *Educational Research: Principles, Policies and Practice*, pp. 97-108. London: Falmer. Retrieved from https://www.actionresearch.net/writings/jack/jw1985analindiv.pdf

Whitehead, J. (1989). Creating a living educational theory from questions of the kind, "How do I improve my practice?'. *Cambridge Journal of Education*, 19(1), pp. 41-52. Retrieved from https://www.actionresearch.net/writings/livtheory.html

Whitehead, J. (1992). How can my philosophy of action research transform and improve my professional practice and produce a good social order? A response to Ortrun Zuber-Skerritt, in Bruce, C. S. & Russell, A. L. (Eds.) *Transforming Tomorrow Today. Proceedings of the Second World Congress on Action Learning*. Queensland; Ron Passfield.

Whitehead, J. (2001). Action Research: research methodology based on field activities. Lecture to the 6th Japan Academy of Diabetes Education, 15 September 2001. Published in 2005 in *The Journal of the Japan Academy of Diabetes Education and Nursing*, 5, pp. 34-37. Retrieved from https://www.actionresearch.net/writings/japan/jwjapandiabetesok.pdf

Whitehead, J. (2003). Creating Our Living Educational Theories in Teaching and Learning to Care: Using Multi-Media to Communicate the Meanings and Influence of our Embodied Educational Values. *Teaching Today for Tomorrow*, 19, pp. 18-22. Retrieved from https://www.actionresearch.net/writings/jack/jwttft2003.pdf

Whitehead, J. (2008). Using a living theory methodology in improving practice and generating educational knowledge in living theories. *Educational Journal of Living Theories*, 1(1), pp. 103-126.

Whitehead, J. (2016). How am I integrating the personal and political in improving professional practice and generating educational knowledge with collaborative/cooperative action research? A paper presented at the CARN 2016 Conference on the 12/11/16) at Bishop Grosseteste University in Lincoln, UK, with the theme of '*Integrating the Personal and Political in Professional Practice*.' Retrieved from https://www.actionresearch.net/writings/carn/jwCARNindividual121116.pdf

Whitehead, J. (2018). *Living Educational Theory research as a way of life*. Bath; Brown Dog Books.

Whitehead, J. (2019). Creating a living-educational-theory from questions of the kind, 'how do I improve my practice?' 30 years on with Living Theory research. *Educational Journal of Living Theories*, 12(2): 1-19.

Retrieved from https://www.actionresearch.net/writings/jack/jwejolts2019.pdf

Whitehead, J. (2020). Contributing to moving action research to activism with Living Educational Theory research. *Canadian Journal of Action Research*, 20(3), pp. 55-73.

Whitehead, J. & Huxtable, M. (2006a). *How are we co-creating living standards of judgement in action-researching our professional practices?* Multi-media text presented at the World Congress of ALARPM and PAR 21-24 August 2006 in Groningen. Retrieved from https://www.actionresearch.net/writings/jack/jwmh06ALARPMmulti.pdf

Whitehead, J. & Huxtable, M. (2006b). *How are we co-creating living standards of judgement in action-researching our professional practices?* Printed text in the Conference Proceedings of the World Congress of ALARPM and PAR 21-24 August 2006 in Groningen. Retrieved from https://www.actionresearch.net/writings/jack/jwmhalarpmtext06.pdf

Whitehead, J. & Rayner, A. (2009). *From Dialectics to Inclusionality: A naturally inclusive approach to educational accountability.* Retrieved from https://www.actionresearch.net/writings/jack/arjwdialtoIncl061109.pdf

Zuber-Skerritt, O. (Ed.) (2017). *Conferences as Sites of Learning and Development: Using Participatory Action Learning and Action Research Approaches.* Abingdon: Routledge.

## Biography

Jack Whitehead is a former President of the British Educational Research Association and Distinguished Scholar in Residence at Westminster College, Utah. He is a Visiting Professor at Ningxia University in China. He is a Visiting Professor of Education at the University of Cumbria. His original contributions to  educational knowledge have focused on the explanations of individuals for their educational influences in learning in enquiries of the kind, 'How do I improve what I am doing?' These contributions can be accessed from his website at http://www.actionresearch.net . He advocates the use of living-posters (http://www.actionresearch.net/writings/posters/homepage020617.pdf ) in developing participatory research programmes.

# How a case study utilizing action learning and action research enhanced public service excellence on a Federal research campus

Christopher Sigle and Emmanuel Tetteh

**Abstract**

*This case study used action learning and action research to examine the ways that the Shared Services Support Program (SSSP) could enhance the primary science mission on a federal research campus. This included the investigation into the role that social capital plays in meeting or exceeding customer expectations. The collaborative efforts of stakeholders' values were also examined as to how they contribute to the effectiveness, efficiency, and improvement of the SSSP. Schalock's (2001) outcome-based evaluative (OBE) case study approach was used within the Participatory Action Research (PAR) framework along with 21 stakeholder participants who provided rich and meaningful data from their extensive experience with the SSSP. The context, input, process, product (CIPP) logic model was used along with Stringer's (2014) Look-Think-Act (LTA) approach as a framework to facilitate data collection and analysis. Five themes emerged: mission support quality, rationale for program patronage, the value of campus shared services, process improvement opportunities, and stakeholder perceived constraints. The findings led to the development of a strategic action plan for SSSP improvement and the promotion of collaborative actions across organizational boundaries.*

**Key words:** Action learning, action research, participatory action research, case study

**What is known about the topic?**

Shared services support programs exist throughout most organizations. However, trends have emerged which threaten these programs and their ability to support the primary mission whether industry or government. Shifting organizational priorities result in various approaches to continued funding of shared services support programs.

**What does this paper add?**

This paper is a result of a case study conducted at a US government federal research campus. The qualitative approach utilized action learning and action research to unearth how social capital theory and public value theory contribute to the sustainment of the shared services support program.

**Who will benefit from its content?**

While this article specifically pertains to the public sector, readers from all sectors and management levels will find the collaborative approach and study outcome of particular interest given how action learning and action research can be applied to improve processes.

**What is the relevance to AL and AR scholars and practitioners?**

The recognition of practical knowledge gained from reflection and evaluation will be readily evident. There is a component to the article which specifically covers critical reflective action learning and activity evaluation that will be of particular interest to scholars and practitioners.

*Received December 2019    Reviewed July 2020    Published December 2020*

# Introduction

Public administrators often struggle to lead organizations that are balancing mission requirements with diminishing resources. This is especially true with mission support organizations. In the context of a federal research campus, mission support includes shared administrative and logistical services that enable the accomplishment of primary scientific functions. To make things more interesting, changing presidential administrations can often bring about new priorities and policy implementations for federal agencies; moreover, this may challenge ongoing work with implications for a shift in organizational mission strategy. These concerns also undergird the work of numerous federal agencies with implications for funding and budgetary concerns (Lane, Evans & Matthews, 2016). When working within the existing resources, leaders do have options for furthering public service excellence by leveraging social capital to enhance public value. This was evidenced using Participatory Action Research (PAR) during a case study involving a federal research and development (R&D) campus (Sigle, 2018).

There is a relationship between social capital and public value as it relates to public service excellence; there are also implications for employee motivation, as well as organizational design, including shared services efficacy (Rothstein, 2012). Much has been written about the public value or social capital, but the literature includes comparatively little on the intersection of the two for impacting mission support within federal agencies. Using qualitative methodology in a PAR case study setting, the authors examined three specific factors regarding a federal R&D organization:

1. The extent to which specific mission support programs are effective in an agency whose primary mission is scientific R&D.

2. The means by which the collaborative efforts of stakeholders' public values can be enhanced using PAR to contribute to the efficacy of mission support programs.

3. The significant roles played by public value and social capital while meeting or exceeding agency customer expectation leading to improved access and utilization of mission support programs and shared services in particular.

## Background and context of practice

This case study examined the ways that the Shared Services Support Program (SSSP) enhanced the primary science mission on a United States federal research campus in Boulder, Colorado. This action research project addressed the improvement of the shared services support program (SSSP) that primarily aids scientific mission support at federal research and development sites (Bontis, Richards & Serenko, 2011; Nagesh & Thomas, 2015). Over the years, reductions in budget and manpower have eroded the foundation of mission support relied upon by scientists, engineers and administrative support personnel. Moreover, changes have resulted in organizational realignments and the corresponding reallocation of fiscal priorities. The SSSP delivery practices are facing challenges due to reductions in their budget and manpower contracts, and feedback from key stakeholders regarding their effectiveness.

The approach included the investigation into the role that three theories intersect to evaluate how the SSSP was meeting or exceeding customer expectations, thereby impacting public value: shared services theory, public value theory, and social capital theory. While contemporary literature focuses substantially on free-market ideology, public value theory, in particular, is the central concept that is augmented with social capital theory to explain the significance of the SSSP as a program that enables the primary science mission. These three theories are interrelated in the structure and context of this case study to illustrate their interdependence for understanding the ways in which the SSSP supports the primary science mission and for identifying process improvement initiatives. The collaborative relationship between service providers and clients defines the nature and success of the SSSP; therefore, it was necessary to include federal employees and contracted personnel throughout the data collection and analysis phases, which contributed to the successful implementation of the conceptual framework. Likewise, the cyclical nature of Stringer's (2014) Look-Think-Act model was utilized with Stufflebeam's logic model (Stufflebeam, 1983) in a Participatory Action Research (PAR) setting for the improvement of the SSSP (see Fig. 1).

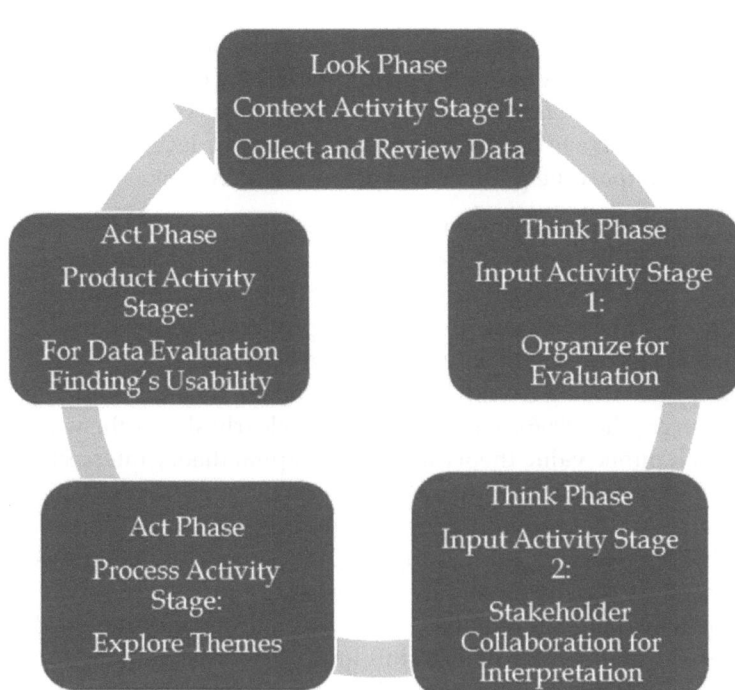

Figure 1: Description of the Case Study Process

## Literature review

Shared services support programs, like many mission support operations, suffer from resource deficiencies, which can impact primary organizational operations (Bergeron, 2002; Grant, McKnight, Uruthirapathy & Brown, 2007). It is therefore likely that mission support programs will be required to adjust to new leadership urgencies throughout the various federal agencies in times of change. For example, changing presidential administrations often result in a changing agenda, corresponding policies, and associated budgets; moreover, this is readily evident with federal scientific research programs (Rubin & Willoughby, 2014). This is also the case for scientific R&D programs at federal campuses that rely on support programs to enable primary mission activity. Lab directors, scientists, engineers, and their support staff all rely on support services that enable them to carry out their day-to-day primary agency missions. Consequently, SSSP managers must be flexible in response to change. This includes looking for ways to improve program efficacy by leveraging social capital to impact the public value of service delivery.

The review of the literature reveals numerous trends for the implementation of shared services throughout the private sector, along with increasing interest in the public sector. Increasing demands for efficiency in government, programs are also driving the expansion of shared services support activities, resulting in a kind of outsourcing from within the organization, or "insourcing" (Janssen & Joha, 2006). The literature also clearly shows the ways in which public value theory and social capital theory intersect with shared services or other mission support activities to depict relationships that promote program success (Baum, MacDougall & Smith, 2006; Harvey, 2013; Stringer, 2014). Budget and manpower increases are conventionally thought of as the cure for program deficiencies, but fiscal realities in today's environment suggest that leadership perspective should shift toward creative thinking to include the means by which social capital can impact public value and drive program improvement.

The SSSP was originally established in 1955 to support a newly created federal research campus in Colorado (see fig. 2). The program has changed the bureau or agency hands numerous times over the past 60 years, but it has remained with the federal agency supporting atmospheric research since the mid-1980s. In 2004, a major reorganization occurred with the unintended consequence of impacting resources over a 12-year period, reducing manpower more than 70% in the area of mission support.

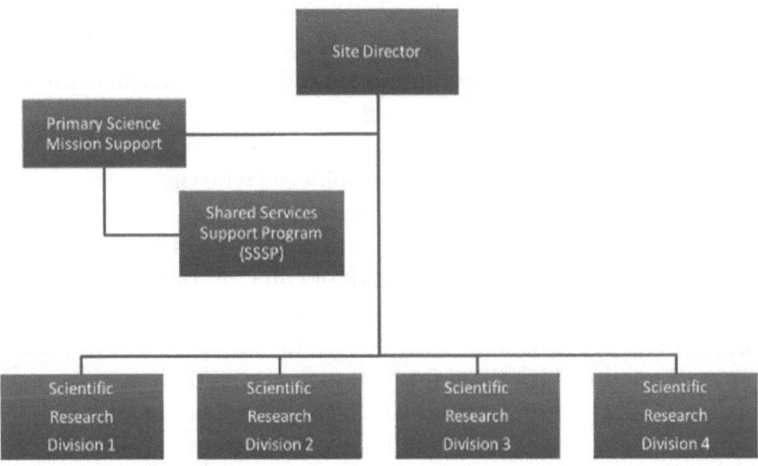

Figure 2: Organizational Chart for Federal Research Campus and SSSP

## Social capital, public value, and participatory action research (PAR)

A review of the literature suggests an apparent need to compare customer needs to public value in view of social capital as they impact mission support service delivery effectiveness (Borman & Janssen, 2013; Dolfsma, 2011). Mandarano, Meenar, and Steins (2010) discuss the implications for social capital as it relates to making choices in the public sector. Likewise, the literature also describes how service quality and trust produce public value (Alkadry, Blessett & Patterson, 2015). This is especially relevant when social networks leverage capital in a variety of transactional activities (Lin, 2008). Consequently, the collaborative actions of stakeholder participants can be leveraged in a PAR setting to baseline an operation, as well as to recommend program improvements (Stringer, 2014).

Social capital theory establishes a connection between shared services theory and public value theory for the purposes of this case study in light of the hypothesized influence of social capital on public value. Yoo (2015) states that innovation is enhanced or furthered through the networks and established relationships maintained or nurtured between employees who operate in a symbiotic environment. Likewise, activity evaluation measures such things as access and utilization to determine efficacy; moreover, stakeholder-service provider collaboration is assumed to be crucial to the success of the SSSP (Besser, 2009; Pearse, 2010; Rothstein, 2012). This case study sought to evaluate the formal and informal relationships that highlight the connection between service delivery providers and clients, as such relationships determine how public value might be enhanced to improve the SSSP. Older paradigms for organizational effectiveness may rely on authoritarian and formal organizational structure or hierarchy, but social capital theory expresses an up-to-date standard for interaction that substantially energizes innovation and continuous improvement.

## Example of shared services

Shared services support programs, like many mission support operations, suffer from resource deficiencies that impact primary organizational operations (Bergeron, 2002; Grant, McKnight, Uruthirapathy & Brown, 2007). This is also true for scientific R&D programs at federal campuses that rely on support programs to enable primary mission activity. Lab directors, scientists, engineers, and their support staff all rely on support services that enable them to carry out their day-to-day primary agency missions. Consequently, SSSP managers must be flexible in response to change. This includes looking for ways to improve program efficacy by leveraging social capital that impacts the public value of service delivery.

Adaptive thinking is required for public program managers when they are faced with shifting resources and new strategic directions (Head & Alford, 2015). As such, recipients of SSSP often express grave concern over the continuation of their projects and programs given the continuous fluctuation within mission support. Consequently, senior leaders frequently look for ways to shore up critical primary mission processes themselves without guarantees that SSSP will continue to be there for them. As such, the collaborative efforts of program recipients and service delivery personnel can make a difference. This is especially evident in the area of shared services, as supported primary missions may be confronted with budget cuts, and support functions must respond in a timely manner with varying levels the service delivery (Burns & Yeaton, 2008). Clients of SSSP have options that sometimes include organic solutions (on-site) or market solutions (off-site); therefore, public program managers must understand the numerous ways that social capital and public value shape client choices while also supporting collaborative action for program improvement. As will be shown in the synopsis of the case study, social capital impacts public value regarding access and utilization of support services.

## Employee motivation

Social capital can influence public value with implications for employee motivation. Public sector motivation relates to public service excellence and often manifests much greater overall job satisfaction (Hur, 2017). This is why federal managers may find cost considerations or financial rewards insufficient as primary methods for encouraging or inspiring employees. Social capital impact on public value; however, it suggests that client-provider relationships go a long way toward wellbeing or morale in the workforce when financial compensation is simply not available to program managers. Accordingly, leaders can find new ways to infuse social capital into the workplace that can have positive effects on choices and behaviors.

Likewise, social capital can serve as a positive motivation for ethical concerns related to integrity. This is especially applicable to the public sector as often the needs of the many results in a collective notion over against individual preferences, thereby viewed as a moral choice (Frederickson, 2010). Frederickson suggests that public sector leaders must recognize and promote a broader understanding of the concepts pertaining to public life as distinct from for-profit activities while building organizational culture and perspective. Ethical concerns, recognition, and reward issues have implications regarding social capital affecting public value. As such, relationship building is essential to program success. Moreover, interpersonal collaboration can be designed into the position itself.

When designing new service deliveries or identifying competencies, one should consider that shared services organization employees often derive great satisfaction from their interaction with customers. The social capital aspect of some jobs may lead employees to choose employment that provides interaction with others. Consequently, leaders should include skill sets emphasizing technical capabilities and social capital for customer focus, as well as leadership or management potential. Human behavior theory suggests that people make choices based on various need levels or while evaluating competing needs; therefore, public sector employees often serve because of public service motivation, which indicates a willingness to put the public interest ahead of personal interest while finding social aspects related to job satisfaction. For example, Victor Vroom's expectancy theory suggests an anticipated outcome pertaining to motivated behavior; additionally, recent research suggests further implications regarding social context (Lloyd & Mertens, 2018). Some, therefore, have observed that motivation is situational; hence, leaders can leverage the unique attributes of the job and engage employees in social capital goal setting while using expectancy theory to help individuals find enthusiastic and meaningful purpose (Shaffer, 2008). Strategic customer service objectives can help with this effort.

Service delivery description must not only consider organizational needs, but also content and process theories of motivation, especially under the circumstances in which these are linked to cultures that value social capital. Numerous theories apply to human resource management as it relates to shared services support operations. For example, dynamic process models describe how individuals interact with their social environment, thus providing a framework for understanding human behavior in intricate situations (Vancouver, 2008). This also provides support for organization leaders, with the potential for analyzing the broad spectrum of operations as they intersect with customer needs and employee behavior. Motivational theoretical frameworks are, therefore, helpful when designing social capital into the fabric of an organizational culture.

Content theories involve a field of motivation theories that endeavor to explain internal factors that drive behavior toward specific goals, whereas process theories propose that employees relate their actions to expected outcomes (Miner, 2015). Consequently, content theories describe needs-based concepts often associated with Maslow, Herzberg, or McClelland, whereas process theories are represented by goal, expectancy, and public-service theories. Position development should incorporate a balance of content and process theories to increase the likelihood of employee job satisfaction, especially when designing a modern workforce with social capital in mind.

A proper assessment of job requirements should begin with the identification of the end result or service delivery objective, with an emphasis on mission needs versus wants. Max Weber skillfully described the description of human institutions, showing how they connect to theories governing political and economic systems; he also proposed that program managers historically used assumed authority to broaden their power base, thereby growing empires with non-essential capabilities (Stillman, 2005). The pendulum has since swung back with the legislative cry for agencies to do more with less, resulting in the need for public leaders to conduct a bottom-up review of operations, thereby distinguishing between nice-to-do and essential activities. Service delivery design must balance desired outcomes with known resource requirements that minimally satisfy mission objectives while looking for variables, such as social capital, that can enhance public value. Likewise, there are implications for performance management, organizational structure, and social capital.

Performance management systems can be successful if organizational leadership is committed (Bush, 2005), but so much depends on the structure of the organization. Elements of the shared services support organization appear to operate as an adhocracy due to the innovative nature of the organization; in addition, it functions in a semi-organic structure and subsists in a fluid communication and social environment (Rainey, 2009). As such, the analysis of this organizational structure suggests a mostly functional orientation that complements the adhocracy where social capital considerations may be essential to consider. Centralization characteristics are important as well.

Andersen and Jonsson (2006) suggest that structure affects the way an organization functions; in turn, the function determines effectiveness. They also propose that other variables include decentralization, affect function. Furthermore, they contend that training and quality leadership have their bearings on effectiveness. Leadership, training, and decentralization variables provide evidence that the assumed cause-and-effect relationship between structure and effectiveness is not a universal absolute. To that end, shared services support program leaders should consider theories that govern structures and effectiveness along with their relation to performance management, while recognizing other relevant factors that also impact organizational effectiveness, such as social capital.

The flexible nature of a shared services support organization is viewed as a strength given the tremendous degree of creativity required. As a weakness, the functional orientation is more rigid, and it sometimes finds itself at odds with the innovative nature of the less rigidly defined configuration. The human element, however, is found in social capital that can mitigate functional structures without sacrificing economics of scale within functional units (Waldman & Jensen, 2016).

## Context

Regarding researcher positionality, the authors' relationship to this case study was that of an outsider with insider's collaboration (O'Sullivan, Rassel & Berner, 2008). As the program manager for mission support, this study was of particular interest for the enhancement of campus research and development support through collaborative action within the framework of an outcome-based case study. Consequently, it was the intention for the authors to leverage research findings not only to fill gaps in the literature but also to produce actionable strategies for campus mission support improvement.

## Methods

The afore-mentioned discussion and broad theoretical framework form the basis for an outcome-based action research case study within the context of PAR. Designing a study to explore how social capital affects public value means action research, and critical reflective action learning might be a preferred approach under the umbrella of qualitative methodology. Therefore, these approaches engender comprehension formation to facilitate experiential understanding as individuals pause and reflect on events (Reynolds & Vince, 2017). It is consequently believed that it is important to organize for reflection to enhance the learning experience. For this, participants collaborated in a concise format comprised of collected and analyzed data made available for key stakeholders to use in the reflection process.

## Design

Using the PAR framework, a collaborative management process of Schalock's (2001) OBE was employed for conducting a case study (Merriam, 1998) of the SSSP. Stringer's (2014) LTA model (see fig. 3) provided the PAR framework using "multiple research techniques aimed at enhancing change and generating data for scientific knowledge production" (Greenwood & Levin, 2007, p. 1). For this, Patton's (2002) approach to methods triangulation played a critical role in conducting the PAR project. Participant stakeholders worked together to facilitate the cyclical LTA process, which enabled knowledge production. Using a collaborative data collection and analysis process, various critical reflective action learning strategies helped to facilitate the PAR project.

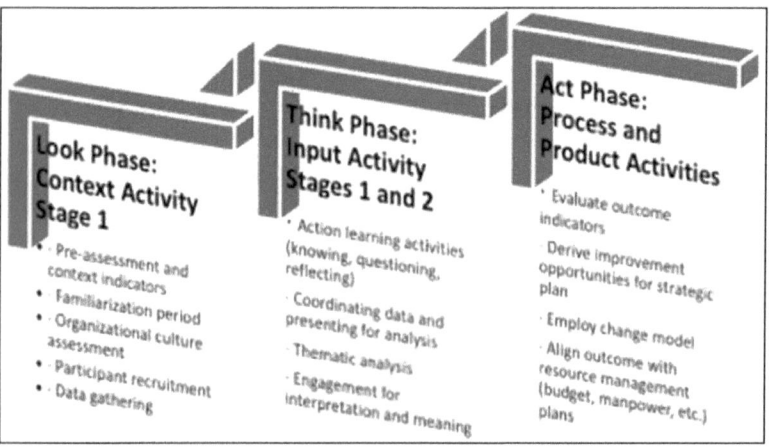

Figure 3: Summary of LTA Activities

This approach was particularly effective in view of Schalock's (2001) OBE model. Schalock contends that seeing is important before believing, which is why the OBE must include data collection and analysis followed by stakeholder interpretation of results for results to be accepted by participant teams. Consequently, reflective learning is a crucial part of this overall OBE process.

Reflective learning provided an opportunity for stakeholder participants to enhance their understanding of the mission support program and its role in supporting the primary agency science mission. Likewise, critical reflective action learning played a key role in understanding important factors pertinent to the success of the program with implications for process improvements.

## Participants, setting, and sampling strategy

This study involved 21 stakeholder participants who were selected based on their historical interaction with the SSSP. Those selected had between five years and 30 years' experience on the federal research campus and had worked with the legacy organization as it had evolved since the reorganization. Specifically, they were enthusiastic about describing mission support before and after the reorganization took place. Using a purposeful sampling approach, participants volunteered for surveys, document reviews, interviews, and focus groups. Stakeholders undertook an action research collaboration activity (see fig. 4).

Figure 4: Action Research Collaboration Model

As described by Greenwood and Levin (2007), the 21 stakeholders participated in a critical reflective action learning process that increased knowledge while motivating transformation and led to program improvements. Participants involved with the SSSP were chosen from the federal organization in Colorado to participate in interviews, a focus group session, and a survey, along with document and record reviews to evaluate their experience with the SSSP based on criteria that included historical context and organizational interaction program patronage. Each participant was a member of either the scientific or engineering community and had relied upon the SSSP for mission support over the years. Likewise, each participant had between five and 30 years of experience on campus describing varying degrees of involvement with the SSSP. Many participants had also worked with the legacy program, which had existed for several decades before the reorganization, lending additional insight to the SSSP. The stakeholders took a keen interest in the study and were enthusiastic about participating in the survey, in-depth interviews, and focus group activities.

## Data collection

Document reviews, surveys, one-on-one interviews, and a focus group produced rich qualitative data for analysis and interpretation. Participant stakeholders found that there was public value to shared services on the R&D campus, but social capital was also seen as a crucial factor for determining the ways that service delivery personnel and customers interacted and the degree to which this interaction impacted access and utilization. Reflective sessions generated additional insight, solidifying the connection between social capital and public value, with implications for increased program effectiveness. Data collection, observation coding, analysis, and interpretation with critical stakeholder participants revealed extensive numbers of comments linking social capital and public value.

Stakeholder participants viewed these as important components of mission support activities as they relate to collaboration, communication, experience, trust, and relationship building/maintenance viewed through the lens of public value and social capital. The data described the means by which scientists and engineers will patron on-site service providers before going off-site, even when variables such as cost and time are considered equal. The impact of social capital on public value is such that patronage of on-site activities equates to several factors best summarized as in the best interest of stewardship of public resources. Time is money, and on-site service providers understand customers' needs based on history, experience, establish relationships, and trust.

## Data analysis

Survey results, interview comments, and a focus group discussion formed the methods triangulation. A total of 417 comments were coded using the Dedoose Online-based Collaborative Data Analysis framework to produce 22 themes under five categories. This collaborative data analysis framework in the PAR setting allowed for the reflection of experiences by participant stakeholders, showing that public value is enhanced by social capital and thereby impacts shared services effectiveness (see fig. 3). These efforts enriched the understanding of the relationship between mission support and primary scientific research success; moreover, these reflective experiences also translated into enhanced mission support with savings to taxpayers.

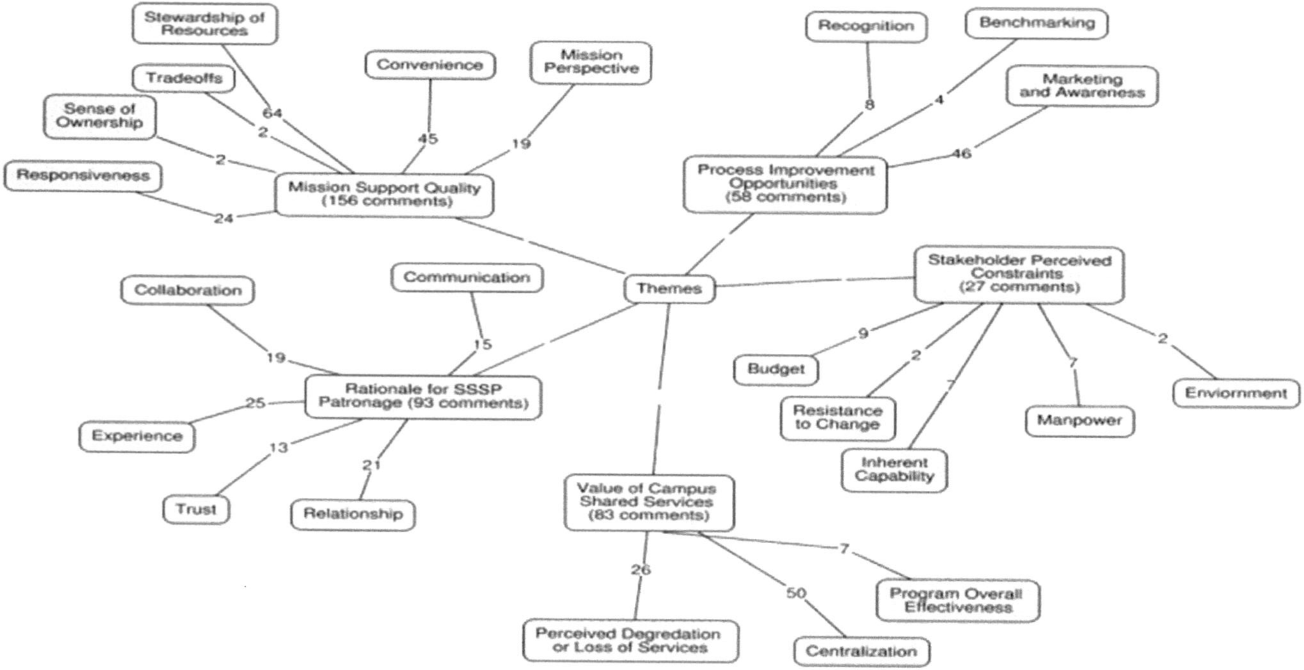

Figure 5: Thematic Analysis of SSSP Effectiveness with Business Process Improvements

# Credibility and action validity in qualitative research

Patton (2002) suggests that prolonged engagement and ongoing collaboration would add to integrity and transparency throughout the case study. The authors were in constant contact with participants and worked collaboratively with stakeholders throughout data collection and analysis. Additionally, Creswell (2014) indicates that action validity was enhanced when knowledge production and transformational change resulted from PAR. Consequently, participants'stakeholders confirmed validity throughout the data analysis phase, whereby the cycle of reflection and interpretation led to collaborative developments all recommendations for program enhancement.

## Findings and results

Case study participants expressed much concern about the mission support organization's ability to support the scientific research and development efforts of the US Department of Commerce Boulder Labs agencies. However, transformative change was evident as participants became more aware of the thematic components supporting the relationship between social capital and public value. This became evident as the nature of PAR played out in the proliferation of ideas for enhancing mission support. In addition to the generation of ideas in the group process leading to more ideas, stakeholders conveyed their appreciation for being a part of the study, anticipating that their involvement could make a positive difference. Their perceptions, beliefs, and values generated a clearer understanding of the way social capital was expressed with relationship building and communication; these factors also enhanced public value, especially when considered regarding convenience and stewardship of resources. With enhanced reflection, stakeholders described how their experiences produced meaning and purposeful interpretation, thus leading to value-added strategic planning inputs. Therefore, this systematic approach provoked growth in stakeholder awareness regarding program effectiveness while generating positive enthusiasm change as evidenced in Table 1 and Figure 3.

Table 1: Coding, Analysis, and Emerging Themes

| Themes | Descriptors | Coding Occurrences |
|---|---|---|
| Mission Support Quality (Relates to public value theory) | Stewardship of resources | 64 |
| | Convenience | 45 |
| | Responsiveness | 24 |
| | Mission perspective | 19 |
| | Tradeoffs | 2 |
| | Sense of ownership | 2 |
| Rationale for SSSP Patronage (Relates to social capital theory) | Experience | 25 |
| | Relationship | 21 |
| | Collaboration | 19 |
| | Communication | 15 |
| | Trust | 13 |
| Value of Shared Services (Relates to Shared Services Theory) | Centralization | 50 |
| | Perceived degradation or loss of services | 26 |
| | Program effectiveness | 7 |
| Process Improvement Opportunities and Constraining Factors | Marketing and awareness | 46 |
| | Recognition | 8 |
| | Benchmarking | 4 |
| | Budget concerns | 9 |
| | Inherent capability | 7 |
| | Manpower concerns | 7 |
| | Environment challenges | 2 |
| | Resistance to change | 2 |

The results of the study illustrated the value of the SSSP for aiding the primary science mission. More than 67% of those surveyed believed that social capital enhanced SSSP public value. Stakeholder participant experience exposed similar findings and concerns, resulting in a common understanding of SSSP dynamics and recommendations for change.

## Discussion and insights gained

This case study effectively integrated 21 participants and six critical stakeholders for exploring how the SSSP supports the primary science mission, investigating how the collaborative efforts of stakeholders' values can be enhanced, contributing to the efficacy of the SSSP, and determining how the public value in social capital plays a role in SSSP patronage. Transformative change was evident, as participants became more aware of the thematic components supporting the relationship between social capital and public value. In addition to the expression of ideas in the group process leading to more ideas, stakeholders also conveyed appreciation for having been a part of the study, anticipating that their involvement could make a positive difference. Their perceptions, beliefs, and values generated a clearer understanding of the way social capital was expressed with relationship building and communication; these factors also enhanced public value, especially when considered in terms of convenience and stewardship of resources. With enhanced reflection, stakeholders described how their experiences produced meaning and purposeful interpretation leading to value-added strategic planning inputs. Thus, this systematic approach provoked growth in stakeholder awareness pertaining to program effectiveness while generating enthusiasm for positive change.

Stakeholder participants devised a strategic action plan to improve campus mission support programs and to promote collaboration across organizational boundaries. Six tasks, all collaboration-oriented in nature, were identified, building upon the gains made throughout the case study. The PAR approach used in triangulation with the OBE and case study were fundamental to the development of new awareness, with positive impacts for organizational culture as it related to the enhancement of public value through social capital and improved mission support program effectiveness.

The following represents how the Action Research and Action Learning cycle was completed.

> Critical reflection and change. While reviewing and interpreting the data, critical stakeholders discerned the emergence of themes with priorities they felt should be addressed to have the greatest impact. Schalock (2001) stated that such findings could relate back to new strategies for change. One participant stakeholder made some relevant observations: "My takeaways from the data are that shared services and centralization are very important highlighting public value. Stewardship of resources goes hand-in-hand with public value, and it's enhanced by having the convenience of the SSSP on site and responsive."
>
> Yet, marketing awareness needs improvement, while experience, relationships, and collaborations are very important as underscored by social capital. Such collaborative relationships will enhance and empower change going forward."
>
> Another reviewed the data, focusing on the enhancement of social capital to promote change with proposed solutions to impact marketing to include the integration of online tools. He stated: "There should be developed a robust online capability and a concise form of marketing which could highlight the mission and vision of the SSSP while also identifying each component of the program with a feedback mechanism, photos of service delivery providers for recognition, and contact information. This should include a two-page handout for quick reference that stakeholders could use to augment the communication process around the SSSP."

Still another participant stakeholder had similar observations: "Data highlighted certain areas where collaborative efforts could be enhanced through marketing, adaptability, and self-service tools. This was pointed out from specifically collected data, indicating a need for greater outreach to customers that could also improve program responsiveness. Marketing initiatives and customer service training could have positive results when it comes to SSSP responsiveness. While we already have an intranet site, periodic campus-wide notices announcing program changes could be helpful."

They also expressed caution with the critical action learning phase, given the necessity for senior leadership review of the study results prior to the implementation of change. Implementation results are summarized in Table 2.

Table 2: Strategic Action Plan for the Improvement of the SSSP

GOAL: Enhance public value through social capital to improve SSSP effectiveness

| Task | Responsibilities | Impact |
|---|---|---|
| Establish SSSP improvement team. | Study leader and key stakeholders | Increased buy-in. |
| Institute customer service council. | Key stakeholders | Enhanced patronage. |
| Integrate customers and service providers. | Key stakeholders and service providers | Improved recognition and ownership. |
| Schedule public event (e.g., open house). | Key stakeholders | Improved program awareness. |
| Deploy marketing strategies. | Key stakeholders | Augmented communication. |
| Adopt technological solutions for self-service capabilities. | Key stakeholders and service providers | Reduced barriers to customer service effectiveness. |

## Thematic findings regarding SSSP support and the literature review

Participants continued to indicate how much they relied on the SSSP throughout the interviews and during the focus group session. Common themes included how budgetary constraints and manpower controls leave their organizational divisions without the ability to perform the support functions for themselves. As the literature implied, many federal organizations operate with a blend of contracted and federal employees, thereby imposing constraints on organic support due to the restrictions of inherently governmental definitions. Various program features were mentioned as important to stakeholders, but centralization was most common, with 50 comments linked to this theme during the coding process. Therefore, there is a greater reliance on the centralization of support capabilities in a shared services context as indicated in the literature, due to the need to eliminate duplication of functionality in federal organizations (Roberts, 2014).

As was shown in the literature review and validated by participants, the SSSP is grounded in public value given that it promotes the stewardship of resources; it is responsive and conveniently located, thereby reducing operational costs while providing foundational and essential mission support (Ramphal, 2013). Patrons repeatedly told the study leader how difficult it would be to go off-site for certain support services given the uniqueness of the requirements stipulating access and utilization on-site; this relates to convenience and stewardship of resources, in most cases, citing savings associated with cost avoidance. Research scientists feel that their time is better spent working with SSSP sources when they consider the cost of their manpower when shopping off-site for mission requirements. Mission planning for scientific expeditions often requires quick logistical solutions for last-minute challenges; again, SSSP solutions are often quicker and, therefore, a better value for the taxpayer. Stakeholders also linked responsiveness to the public value given that off-site market solutions do not always relate to customer satisfaction and timeliness of mission requirement fulfillment.

## Thematic findings regarding the enhancement of public value and the literature review

Business practices are considered efficient in the public sector and deemed to provide public value when they are responsive to the needs of society as described by the literature (Rutgers & Overeem, 2014; Try & Radnor, 2007). Interview and focus group participants, however, expressed frustration with systems beyond their control. Mission support activities are sometimes delayed or terminated due to events abroad. One illustration includes materials being held up in foreign ports due to international customs issues and scientific operations clients relying on SSSP service delivery providers to expedite processes, thereby moving the expedition or project forward. Still, these services and other SSSP functions benefit from the constant interaction between clients and service delivery providers, thereby enabling continuous process improvement initiatives. The implications for the enhancement of public value continue with the leveraging of trust, as evidenced by the literature when considering the collaborative actions of stakeholder participants through meaningful engagement (Suárez & Hokyu, 2008). Clients have choices for off-site market solutions, but the relationships and developed trust lend support to the decision-making process for SSSP patronage. Participants implied that social capital enhances the public value and is further substantiated in the willingness of customers and service delivery providers to partner together for the ongoing promotion of program efficacy.

## Thematic findings regarding the SSSP patronage and the literature review

Participant stakeholders consistently communicated their support for program effectiveness and acknowledged their growth throughout this participatory action research case study. This eventuality is significant, as it aligns with the expectations of the literature, which described how an evaluator develops relationships with stakeholders, with the end-result leveraging expertise and the expansion of professional competence (Rossi, Lipsey, & Freeman, 2004). Moreover, they matured their overall understanding of the SSSP inner workings by having been involved in the identification of major themes, definition of study objectives, scope clarification, data collection, and analysis and interpretation with meaning (Fitzpatrick, Sanders, & Worthen, 2011). The enthusiasm generated by the study among stakeholder participants, therefore, was beneficial to their development and crucial to the identification of process for the improvement of opportunities, identification of constraints, or challenges and creative solutions for overcoming obstacles.

## Contextual summary of the action learning reflection

Action research and action learning worked well together when integrated with the outcome-based evaluation framework, thereby assembling an in-depth awareness of SSSP components and an understanding of how well the SSSP supports the primary science mission with actionable program improvement recommendations. Interviewees and focus group participants built upon the findings of survey results and document reviews when concluding that the site population needs greater visibility of program offerings. Their responses included:

- One study participant indicated, "The director's council isn't providing the trickle-down of information needed with regards to the SSSP. Not enough people are talking about the services [we] are doing, and I've just had to figure things out on the fly."

- A second participant suggested that "There may be physical or electronic enhancements of many kinds. I can make it more worthwhile for browsing program services."

- Another noted, "There may be opportunities for committees to form with marketing and benchmarking in mind so as to better socialize program capabilities an awareness."

This was readily evident as stakeholder participants interacted with one another while exploring the SSSP from several different perspectives, resulting in an exchange of opinions with greater quality solutions offered for process improvement consideration.

Stakeholder participants agreed that their wealth of experience was beneficial to the case study overall, especially as it relates to the quality of data collected and findings with rich interpretation. They also expressed caution with the critical action learning phase, given the necessity for senior leadership review of the study results prior to the implementation of change.

## Conclusion

The results of the study illustrated the value of the SSSP toward aiding the primary science mission. The results added to the body of knowledge and also confirmed theories regarding shared services and public value. The study also engaged participant stakeholders using an OBE in an action research setting, thereby greatly enhancing study results while generating energy and enthusiasm for change. Given the challenges facing this bureau on the national level in areas of mission support, there is a high degree of probability that this study will be reviewed to shed light on systems and processes for enhancement through collaborative action.

## References

Alkadry, M. G., Blessett, B. & Patterson, V. L. (2015). Public administration, diversity, and the ethic of getting things done. *Administration & Society*, 0095399715581032.

Andersen, J. & Jonsson, P. (2006). Does organization structure matter? On the relationship between the structure, functioning and effectiveness. *International Journal of Innovation & Technology Management*, 3(3), pp. 237–263.

Baum, F., MacDougall, C. & Smith, D. (2006). Participatory action research. *Journal of Epidemiology and Community Health*, 60(10), 854. http://dx.doi.org.library.capella.edu/10.1136/jech.2004.028662.

Bergeron, B. (2002). *Essentials of shared services* (Vol. 26). John Wiley & Sons.

Besser, T. L. (2009). Changes in small town social capital and civic engagement. *Journal of Rural Studies*, 25(2), pp. 185-193. 10.1016/j.jrurstud.2008.10.005.

Bontis, N., Richards, D. & Serenko, A. (2011). Improving service delivery. *The Learning Organization*, 18(3), p. 239. 10.1108/09696471111123289.

Borman, M. & Janssen, M. (2013). Reconciling two approaches to critical success factors: The case of shared services in the public sector. *International Journal of Information Management*, 33(2), pp. 390–400. 10.1016/j.ijinfomgt.2012.05.012.

Burns, T. J. & Yeaton, K. G. (2008). *Success factors for implementing shared services in government*. Washington, DC: IBM Center for the Business of Government.

Bush, P. (2005). Strategic performance management in government: Using the balanced scorecard. *Cost Management*, 19(3), pp. 24–31.

Creswell, J. W. (2014). *A concise introduction to mixed methods research*. Thousand Oaks, CA: Sage.

Dolfsma, W. (2011). Government failure: Four types. *Journal of Economic Issues*, 45(3), pp. 593–604.

Fitzpatrick, J. L., Sanders, J. R. & Worthen, B. R. (2011). *Program evaluation: Alternative approaches and practical guidelines* (4th ed.). Boston, MA: Pearson.

Frederickson, H. (2010). Searching for virtue in the public life: Revisiting the vulgar ethics thesis. *Public Integrity*, 12(3), pp. 239–246. doi:10.2753/PIN1099-9922120303 .

Grant, G., McKnight, S., Uruthirapathy, A. & Brown, A. (2007). Designing governance for shared services organizations in the public service. *Government Information Quarterly*, 24(3), pp. 522–538.

Greenwood, D. J. & Levin, M. (2007). An epistemological foundation for action research. *Introduction to action research*, pp. 55-76. Thousand Oaks, CA: Sage.

Harvey, M. (2013). So you think you are doing action research? Indicators of enactment of participatory action research in higher education. *Action Learning and Action Research Journal*, 19(1),p. 115.

Head, B. W. & Alford, J. (2015). Wicked problems: Implications for public policy and management. *Administration & Society*, 47(6), pp. 711–739.

Hur, Y. (2017). Testing Herzberg's two-factor theory of motivation in the public sector: Is it applicable to public managers? *Public Organization Review*, 18, pp. 329–343.

Janssen, M., & Joha, A. (2006). Motives for establishing shared service centers in public administrations. *International Journal of Information Management*, 26(2), pp. 102–115.

Lane, N. F., Evans, K. M., & Matthews, K. R. (2016). *The vital role of the White House Office of Science and Technology Policy in the new administration*. Retrieved from http://hdl.handle.net/1911/92696.

Lin, N. (2008). A network theory of social capital. *Handbook of Social Capital*, 50(1), p. 69.

Lloyd, R., & Mertens, D. (2018). Expecting more out of expectancy theory: History urges inclusion of the social context. *International Management Review*, 14(1), pp. 28-43.

Mandarano L., Meenar, M., & Steins, C. (2010). Building social capital in the digital age of civic engagement. *Journal of Planning Literature*, 25(2), pp. 123-135, doi:10.1177/0885412210394102.

Merriam, S. B. (1998). *Qualitative research and case study applications in education. Revised and expanded from case study research in education*. San Francisco: Jossey-Bass Publishers.

Miner, J. B. (2015). *Organizational behavior 1: Essential theories of motivation and leadership*. New York: Routledge.

Nagesh, D. S., & Thomas, S. (2015). Success factors of public funded R&D projects. *Current Science* (00113891), 108(3), 357-363.

O'Sullivan, E., Rassel, G. R., & Berner, M. (2008). *Research methods for public administrators*. Upper Saddle River, NJ: Pearson.

Patton, M. Q. (2002). Two decades of developments in qualitative inquiry: A personal, experiential perspective. *Qualitative social work*, 1(3), pp. 261-283.

Pearse, N. J. (2010). Towards a social capital theory of resistance to change. *Journal of Advances in Management Research*, 7(2), pp. 163-175.

Ramphal, R. (2013). A literature review on shared services. *African Journal of Business Management*, 7(1), pp. 1-7.

Rainey, H. G. (2009). *Understanding and managing public organizations* (4th ed.). San Francisco, CA: Jossey-Bass.

Reynolds, M., Vince, R., & ProQuest Ebooks. (2016; 2017). *Organizing reflection* (1st ed.). New York, NY: Routledge. 10.4324/9781315247502.

Roberts, J. B. (2014). Inherently governmental functions: A bright line rule obscured by the fog of war. *The Army Lawyer*, 3-24. Retrieved from http://library.capella.edu/login?qurl=https%3A%2F%2Fsearch.proquest.com%2Fdocview%2F1540957073%3Faccountid%3D27965

Rossi, P. H., Lipsey, M. W., & Freeman, H. E. (2004). *Evaluation: A systematic approach* (7th ed.). Thousand Oaks, CA: Sage.

Rothstein, B. (2012). *Political legitimacy for public. The Sage handbook of public administration.* pp. 407–419. Thousand Oaks, CA: Sage.

Rubin, M. M., & Willoughby, K. G. (2014). Measuring government performance: The intersection of strategic planning and performance budgeting. In *Developments in Strategic and Public Management*, pp. 41-58. Palgrave Macmillan, London.

Rutgers, M. R., & Overeem, P. (2014). Public values in public administration. *Journal of Public Administration Research and Theory*, 24(3), pp. 806–812, https://doi.org/10.1093/jopart/muu017.

Schalock, R. L. (2001). *Outcome-based evaluation.* New York, NY: Plenum.

Schaffer, B. (2008). Leadership and motivation. *SuperVision*, 69(2), pp. 6–10.

Sigle, C. L. (2018). *Collaborative action for shared services' support program improvement: Outcome-based evaluative case study* (Order No. 10843798). Retrieved from http://library.capella.edu/login?qurl=https%3A%2F%2Fsearch.proquest.com%2Fdocview%2F2089050122%3Faccountid%3D27965.

Stillman, R. J., II (Ed.). (2005). *Public administration: Concepts and cases* (8th ed.). Boston: Houghton Mifflin.

Stringer, E. T. (2014). *Action research* (4th ed.). Thousand Oaks, CA: Sage.

Stufflebeam, D. L. (1983). *Systematic evaluation.* Boston, MA: Kluwer-Nijhoff. doi:10.1007/978-94-009-5656-8.

Suárez, D. F., & Hwang, H. (2008). Civic engagement and nonprofit lobbying in California, 1998-2003. *Nonprofit and Voluntary Sector Quarterly*, 37(1), pp. 93–112. 10.1177/0899764007304467.

Try, D., & Radnor, Z. (2007). Developing an understanding of results-based management through public value theory. *International Journal of Public Sector Management*, 20(7), pp. 655–673.

Vancouver, J. (2008). Integrating self-regulation theories of work motivation into a dynamic process theory. *Human Resource Management Review*, 18(1), pp. 1–18.

Waldman, D., & Jensen, E. (2016). *Industrial organization: Theory and practice.* New York, NY: Routledge.

Yoo, D. K. (2015, January). Innovation: Its relationships with a knowledge sharing climate and interdisciplinary knowledge integration in cross-functional project teams. In *System Sciences (HICSS), 2015 48th Hawaii International Conference*, pp. 3750-3759). IEEE.

# Biographies

Dr. Christopher Sigle is a faculty member in the Master of Public Administration program with Norwich University. Since 2010, he has been working for the National Oceanic and Atmospheric Administration (NOAA) in Boulder, Colorado. He is also currently Chairman of the Colorado Federal Executive Board.

He completed his undergraduate degree with Texas A&M Commerce and Master of Public Administration (MPA) degree at Troy State University. In 2018, he completed a Doctorate in Public Administration (DPA) degree at Capella University. The dissertation involved a "Collaborative Action for Shared Services' Support Program Improvement: Outcome-Based Evaluative Case Study." The topic relates to public service excellence with a focus on public value, social capital and shared services.

Dr. Emmanuel Tetteh is a faculty member in the MPA program at Norwich University, Grand Canyon University, Metropolitan College of New York (MCNY), and in the School of Business at Mercy College. He served as a faculty member at Capella University, where he taught and mentored doctoral candidates. He holds a BPS degree in Human Services and MS degree in Administration from MCNY, and a Ph.D.  degree in Public Policy and Administration from Walden University. He has authored journal articles and peer-reviewed books, including workshop presentations at international conferences. He recently developed an internet of things (IoT) action-learning solution model of big data policy-analytic epistemology published in the Handbook of Research on Big Data and the IoT. Through action learning/action research (AL/AR), and program evaluation projects, Dr. Tetteh coined the metaphor of the "Communal Photosynthesis (CP)" phenomenon. He also developed an intriguing AL model grounded in the systemic thinking of his CP metaphor and introduced the "creative-reflective methodology" unraveling the *Identify, Act, Reflect, Evaluate,* and *Produce* (IAREP) model for participatory action research. As of 2013, He has maintained a unanimous election as the International Vice President of Action Learning, Action Research Association Ltd (ALARA).

# An action learning intervention on work-family balance

John Molineux, Rodney Carr and Adam Fraser

## Abstract

*The purpose of this paper is to explore the impact of an action learning intervention using positive psychological techniques to impact work-family balance. It draws on theory and practice from positive psychology and action learning interventions. The research reported in this paper is exploratory in nature and utilizes a positive psychological intervention, the Third Space, with several organizational groups. Participants in the groups were given time to discuss and operationalize their ideas about it with colleagues, and then commit to take action appropriate to their work and family contexts. Survey data was gathered from attendees prior to workshops and again approximately five weeks after the workshops. The results suggest that, on average, exposure to the ideas in the workshops may have led employees to develop a more positive mind-state and improved perception of work-family balance.*

**Key words:** Positive psychology, mindfulness, intervention, action learning, mind-state, work-family balance, boundary theory

| What is known about the topic? |
|---|
| The Third Space technique reported in this article is related to positive psychological techniques including detachment, mindfulness and work-life segmentation |

> **What does this paper add?**
> The paper shows that it is possible to use action learning in workshops to influence work-family balance through altered mind-states about separation of work and home
>
> **Who will benefit from its content?**
> Organisational managers that are concerned about their employees work and family balance would benefit by understanding The Third Space process and utilising it within their workplaces
>
> **What is the relevance to AL and AR scholars and practitioners?**
> The paper shows AL and AR scholars another example of the use of action learning in improving outcomes for individuals

*Received February 2020     Reviewed November 2020     Published December 2020*

# Introduction

How does a worker transition from work to home and not let problems in the work environment impact aspects of life in the home domain? The impact of work spilling over into the home domain is often a negative one; things that happen at work can spill over to the home environment and result in conflict (Greenhaus & Beutell, 1985). Sources of conflict include job stress, excessive job demands and the need to bring work home (Grzywacz & Marks, 2000; Grotto & Lyness, 2010). The effects can be observed in a worker's behaviour at home and potentially also impact their partner's wellbeing (Grotto & Lyness, 2010; Sanz-Vergel, Rodríguez-Muñoz, Bakker, & Demerouti, 2012).

There are many strategies that can reduce the extant to which work spills over into home and family life. For example, supervisory support and organizational support can reduce the impact of role conflict (Cegarra-Leiva, Sánchez-Vidal, & Cegarra-Navarro, 2012; McCarthy, Cleveland, Hunter, Darcy, & Grady, 2013; Fiksenbaum, 2014). The present research is concerned with another strategy: exposing workers to ideas from positive psychology (Seligman & Csikszentmihalyi, 2000). More specifically, we investigate the efficacy of using action learning intervention workshops (Revans, 1982, 2011), in which workers are exposed to and explore ideas from positive psychology and how they might use them during the transition period from work to home to improve their mind-state arriving home. If workers do arrive home in a more positive state of mind, the expectation is that they enjoy a better work-family balance.

## Work-family balance

Work-family balance (WFB) is a concept that fits under the general umbrella of work-life balance, but, as the name implies, is focussed on aspects of the way work and family-life relate to one another. Grzywacz and Carlson (2007, p. 458) define WFB as the "accomplishment of role-related expectations that are negotiated and shared between an individual and his or her role-related partners in the work and family domains". Similarly, Maertz and Boyar (2011) suggest that WFB for individuals is their perceived fit among role responsibilities, boundaries, values and environmental demands, incorporating their preference for integration or segmentation of roles. Wayne, Butts, Casper and Allen (2017) note the importance of individual balance satisfaction and balance effectiveness. However, the concept is quite subjective; one person's view of a balance between their work and family roles could be quite different to another person's. Leslie, King and Clair (2019) suggest that these perceptions are influenced by individuals' own ideologies of work and life, based on their personal contexts of organization, family, community and society, plus personal work-life preferences and experiences. In the present research, we use WFB, appropriately operationalized, as the main output variable.

The following sections explore the concepts and strategies in the extant literature from which the contents of the action learning workshops were developed.

## Strategies to reduce negative spillover of work and improve WFB

Some strategies to reduce negative spillover are extrinsic to the worker, such as the supervisory and organizational support mentioned previously, but this paper focuses on more intrinsic strategies. They include cognitive and behavioural strategies and coping style and skills. Many are derived from ideas of positive psychology (Seligman & Csikszentmihalyi, 2000), mindfulness (Hahn, 1976, Kabat-Zinn, 1994) and psychological detachment (Etzion, Eden, & Lapidot, 1998), and many are known to be effective. For example, Byron (2005, p. 190) found that coping style and skills "seemed to offer some benefit to employees [and] those with better time management skills or a better coping style tended to have less WIF [work-interference-with-family]". Other strategies that have been shown to be effective include: resting or taking a break (Demerouti, Bakker, Sonnentag, & Fullagar, 2012); acceptance (Britt, Crane, Hodson, & Adler, 2016); getting help from other people (Hyman, Scholarios, & Baldry, 2005); meeting friends (Sonnentag, 2001); arranging time to fit in with family (Zheng, Kashi, Fan, Molineux., & Ee, 2016); and allowing boundary permeability such as maintaining an emotional boundary from work, but letting work correspondence through (Kreiner, Hollensbe, & Sheep, 2009).

The action learning intervention workshops investigated in this research focus on intrinsic strategies associated with recovery experiences that workers can use during the transition time between work and home. Examples of these include the 'kick back and relax' and 'take time for leisure' techniques noted by Sonnentag and Fritz (2007, p. 213). They also include strategies such as: psychological detachment – mentally switching off from work (Etzion et al 1998); relaxation-oriented strategies, such as meditation, walking in a natural environment, listening to music (Sianoja, Syrek, de Bloom, Korpela, & Kinnunen (2018); personal control during leisure time (Bosch, Sonnentag, & Pinck, 2018); and diversionary activities such as immersion in hobbies, sharing information about work immediately and then moving to other topics, and developing rituals such as not accessing work emails at home (Sonnentag, Kuttler, & Fritz, 2010). Other recovery-type strategies that workers might use include physical activities, such as exercise, physical training and sport (Bakker, Demerouti, Oerlemans, & Sonnentag, 2013) or spending time on social and low-effort activities (ten Brummelhuis & Bakker, 2012).

## Positive psychology, mindfulness, psychological detachment, and segmentation

Positive psychology arose from the work of Csikzentmihalyi (1988, 1990, 2003) and Seligman (1994). It is a wide-ranging theory, but in our context it suggests that explicit expression of positive emotions both at work and at home may reduce negative spillover and enhance any positive impacts of work into the home domain (Sanz-Vergel, Demerouti, Moreno-Jiménez, & Mayo, 2010; Daniel & Sonnentag, 2014). Rotondo and Kincaid (2008) found that such positive thinking was associated with higher work-family facilitation and they suggested that positive thinking may have a role in achieving WFB by increasing facilitation and positive spillover. In one four week experimental study, Sheldon and Lyubormirsky (2006) found that three positive thinking mental exercises produced reductions in negative affect and one of these (visualizing best possible selves) also increased positive affect in participants.

Mindfulness developed from work such as Hahn (1976) and Kabat-Zinn (1994) and is based on meditation techniques (Goleman & Schwartz, 1976). It has been associated with the self-regulation of chronic pain (Kabat-Zinn, Lipworth, & Burney, 1985) and the reduction of stress (Kabat-Zinn, Massion, Kristeller, Peterson, Fletcher, Pbert, & et al., 1992). It is the ability to reduce stress, in particular work-stress, and effects on WFB in which we are most interested. This builds upon work such as Michel, Bosch and Rexroth (2014) who showed mindfulness influenced work-family conflict, work-life balance and psychological detachment.

Psychological detachment is a concept introduced by Etzion et al. (1998). Sanz-Vergel, Demerouti, Bakker and Moreno-Jiménez (2011, p. 777) describe it as "off-job activities that help to achieve recovery, including psychological detachment from work, relaxation, mastery experiences, and control over leisure time". Moreno-Jiménez, Mayo, Sanz-Vergel, Geurts, Rodríguez-Muñoz and Garros (2009, p. 435) found support that psychological detachment from work "effectively mitigates some of the negative effects of WFC [work-family conflict] on employees' well-being".

Sanz-Vergel et al. (2011) found that detaching from work increased evening cognitive liveliness and reduced work-home interference. Similar findings were made by Sonnentag, Binnewies and Mojza (2008), and Park, Fritz and Jex (2011, p. 464) found that "creating a sense of segmentation can help people mentally detach from work and recover from work stress". Sonnentag and Bayer (2005) found that people who detached psychologically from work during leisure time reported more positive mood and less fatigue. Such cross-role interruption behaviours may relate to physical barriers or, more likely given the focus on 'presence', to the creation of psychological barriers (Sonnentag, 2012).

According to boundary theory (Nippert-Eng, 1996), people use boundary management strategies to define and organise, or segment, their lives into the different realms of work and home (Kossek, Noe, & DeMarr, 1999). For example, some people turn off their work phones when at home, others may only look at work emails after children are in bed. The strategies vary with the individual preferences of people for integration or segmentation of these realms (Ashforth, Kreiner, & Fugate, 2000; Olson-Buchanan & Boswell 2006; Park et al., 2011). Kossek, Ruderman, Braddy and Hannum (2012) identified that cross-role interruptions involved breaks in the journey from work to home, such as social activities and exercise activities. Effective segmentation of work and home can lead to significant benefits in reducing work-life conflict and attaining a better sense of work-life balance of individuals (Kreiner, 2006; Olsen-Buchanan & Boswell, 2006).

These theories and practices from positive psychology have informed the creation of the action learning workshops as described in detail in the method section.

### Work-life training interventions

Work-life interventions are defined by Kossek (2016, p. 244) as those that are aimed at "reducing work-life and work-family conflicts in order to enhance the well-being and effectiveness of employees and their families, and the organisations in which they work". Although this definition includes a broad range of interventions from flexible work options to support and training, the focus of the present study is on interventions using action learning techniques.

Different types of work group training interventions can be used for helping employees develop positive thinking and detachment strategies. For example, Sanz-Vergel et al. (2011) investigated training programs to teach employees about detaching work and home. Sonnentag and Grant (2012) called for coaching programs that teach employees how to build daily routines in positive thinking. Hammer, Kossek, Anger, Bodner & Zimmerman (2011) identified advantages in conducting such workshops for groups rather than providing individually focused training, at least for some types of employees. In experimental research, Michel et al. (2014) used a program teaching mindfulness as a boundary segmentation technique to improve work-life balance.

The strategies employed in the action learning intervention workshop studied in this research are similar to others used in previous studies. However, one feature of the workshop is that it is designed to specifically target workers' mind-state. This is discussed in the following section, with further details about the action learning intervention workshop provided in the Methods section below.

### Proposed mediating variable: Mind-state

Mind-state is described as positive states of mind by Horowitz, Adler and Kegeles (1988) and Adler, Horowitz, Garcia and Moyer (1998) and includes: focused attention; productivity; and responsible caretaking. For example, an individual who may have experienced a stressful day at work and feels some distress, may choose their 'mind-state' to focus on the family when returning home from work, and in that choice detach from work-related issues. Mind-state is a concept related to mood, but is less persistent (cf. Van Wijhe, Peeters and Schaufeli (2011) with Hamilton, Vohs, Sellier and Meyvis (2011)). In the present research Mind-state is proposed as the mechanism via which any effects due to the action learning intervention workshop on WFB are mediated.

As mentioned previously, the action learning workshop focused on participants' use of the transition time between work and home. It also involves critical reflection on their mind-state on arrival from home and the notion of being 'present' for family members and how they 'show up' when arriving at home. These are similar to strategies studied by Jain, Shapiro, Swanick, Roesch, Mills, Bell and Schwartz (2007), who found they had a positive effect on mind-state. The workshop also includes aspects of mindfulness, but this approach differs from other interventions around mindfulness (e.g. Josefsson, Lindwall, & Bromberg, 2014) that mostly consist of training in meditation techniques. Instead, the workshop uses story-telling, followed by small group discussion and action planning.

The present action learning intervention may result in decisions by individuals to change behavior, particularly impacting on their transition from work to home through tangible measures such as clarifying boundaries between roles (Kossek et al., 1999) and using transitions between roles (Ashforth et al., 2000) to enter subsequent roles in a positive psychological state. This would be indicated by their entry into the home environment from work through a more focused mind-state and a preparedness to be 'present' towards family members.

The above suggests that the action learning workshop intervention should enable workers being able to focus on maintaining a positive mind-state on arrival at home, which suggests the following research question:

RQ1: Can an action learning workshop intervention improve the mind-state of workers on arrival at home?

## Proposed impact of the action learning intervention on WFB

As discussed in the previous section, we expect the impact of the action learning intervention on WFB to be mostly mediated by the mind-state variable. Thus:

RQ2: Does an improvement in mind-state on arriving at home also improve perception of work-family balance?

In addition to an indirect effect via mind-state, we allow for a direct effect of the action learning intervention on WFB in our proposed model. This is similar to the approach taken by Michel et al. (2014) in their experimental research mentioned earlier. We also allow for effects due to demographic variables. Figure 1 shows the proposed research model.

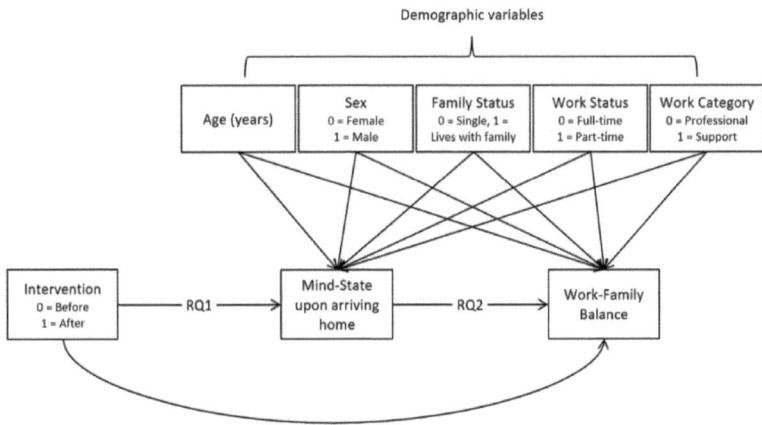

Fig. 1: Proposed research model

## Method

### Participants and procedure

The action learning intervention workshops were organised as part of on-site work conferences for four different organisations based in Australia and New Zealand. These conferences were held for business purposes, and the Third Space intervention was the only discussion about WFB or positive psychology within these conferences. It is also the only common link between them. Prior to each workshop participants were informed about the project and ethics requirements. Those consenting to participate in the research completed a questionnaire about their current work-life transitions and feelings in relation to returning home from work. For the first and third groups of participants, the questionnaire was paper-based and completed just prior to the workshop; the second and fourth groups of participants completed the questionnaire online in the week before the workshop. This was due to the requirements of the host organisations. Participants then attended the action learning workshop intervention. One month later, participants were sent an email with a link to an on-line questionnaire. Reminders were sent approximately another two weeks later. The second questionnaire asked participants the same questions as in the first questionnaire, with a few additional open-ended questions asking them to describe any changes they felt had taken place since the workshop. To encourage participation, both questionnaires were completed anonymously; as a consequence matching of data pre- and post-intervention for individual participants was not possible. This meant that the design is neither a between-subjects design (because the same participants completed the questionnaires) nor a within-subjects (repeated measures) design. This limits the types of statistical analysis that can be employed to descriptive techniques; no inferential techniques can be employed that might allow generalisation of the results.

Table 1 summarises information for the four groups of participants. Only questionnaires that contained responses to all relevant questions were declared useable – no data imputation techniques were used.

| Description | Number of useable pre-intervention responses | Emails sent by | Number of useable post-intervention responses |
|---|---|---|---|
| Group 1 Small business owners and employees across Australia from a small business franchising organisation. | 95 | Research team | 29 (31%) |
| Group 2 Managers and senior employees from a large retail organisation based in New Zealand. | 87 | Employer | 50 (57%) |
| Group 3 Administration and school support staff from a public education department based in Australia. | 395 | Employer | 139 (35%) |
| Group 4 Professional people belonging to an association based in Australia. | 36 | The association | 12 (33%) |
| Total | 613 | | 230 (37%) |

Table 1: Summary of groups participating in the research

Notes: Group 3 consists of two separate and similar-sized workshop groups from the one organisation. All 613 participants who filled in the pre-intervention survey attended one of the action learning workshops.

Table 2 summarises demographic information for the participants. The sample is clearly not representative of the general population in relation to age and gender, however, previous research in this area has found that demographics such as age and gender often have little impact (e.g. see Byron, 2005; Allen, Johnson, Saboe, Cho,

Dumani, & Evans, 2012). However, other demographic variables or personality-type factors that we did not measure probably did influence individuals' decisions to participate in this survey; there is likely to be some self-selection bias, especially with regards to participation in the post-intervention survey. For example, the level of affective commitment to the organisation (Allen and Meyer, 1990) may affect a workshop participant's decision to complete the second questionnaire. Since variables such as these were not measured, methods for correcting for self-selection bias, such as those described in Cuddeback, Wilson, Orme and Combs-Orme (2004), could not be applied.

| Variable | Category | Pre-test | Post-test |
|---|---|---|---|
| Age | 18-29 years (coded as 24.5) | 25 (4.1%) | 12 (5.2%) |
| | 30-39 years (coded as 34.5) | 78 (12.7%) | 27 (11.7%) |
| | 40-49 years (coded as 44.5) | 196 (32.0% | 69 (30.0%) |
| | 50-59 years (coded as 54.5) | 246 (40.1%) | 102 (44.3%) |
| | 60 years or more (coded as 70) | 68 (11.1%) | 20 (8.7%) |
| | All | 613 (100%) | 230 (100%) |
| Gender | Female (= 0) | 505 (82.4% | 189 (82.2%) |
| | Male (= 1) | 108 (17.6%) | 41 (17.8%) |
| | All | 613 (100%) | 230 (100%) |
| Family status | Not living with family or partner (= 0) | 54 (8.8%) | 16 (7.0%) |
| | Living with family or partner (= 1) | 559 (91.2%) | 214 (93.0%) |
| | All | 613 (100%) | 230 (100%) |
| Work status | Full-time (= 0) | 478 (78.0%) | 189 (82.2%) |
| | Part-time (= 1) | 135 (22.0%) | 41 (17.8%) |
| | All | 613 (100%) | 230 (100%) |
| Work category | Professional (= 0) | 203 (33.1%) | 78 (33.9%) |
| | Support (= 1) | 410 (66.9%) | 152 (66.1%) |
| | All | 613 (100%) | 230 (100%) |

Table 2: Summary of demographic variables

## The 'Third Space' intervention

The intervention was a three-hour group action learning workshop in which participants were exposed to the The Third Space concept (Fraser, 2012) and how this related to their own lives and experiences. A diagram summarising The Third Space concept is presented in Figure 2.

Fig. 2: The Third Space

The workshops were all facilitated by the third author. In the workshop, issues and some crisis stories related to WFB were presented. For example, a story was told of a professional who comes home from work and has not separated work from home. Instead of arriving as parent, the individual arrives in work mode and starts organising the partner and children, as well as often being interrupted with work calls. Another story was of a parent who arrives home every work day too late to greet the children. The impact over time on the relationship with the children and partner was then discussed.

In Figure 2, the First Space was discussed primarily as work and the Second Space as home. The Third Space was discussed as the transition time between moving from one life role to the other. The recommended process of reflection activities (Reflect, Rest, Reset) was then outlined, including critical questions about being fully 'present' (related to mindfulness) when you arrive at home, and in what mind-state you 'show-up' to greet family members (related to creating a sense of detachment from work). Figure 2 includes three reflective techniques, including several self-reflective questions. Participants were also presented with a range of ideas on how to segment their work and home responsibilities by prioritising family over work in home situations, and in modifying the way work is done within the home environment (related to segmentation). Participants were then told stories about people who have been able to improve their own situations using these techniques, followed with small group discussions about how The Third Space techniques may be able to assist participants' own situations. Participants were encouraged to reflect on their own behaviour and discuss this with other participants. This design allowed the participants to use action learning techniques such as those outlined in Marquandt, Skipton Leonard, Freedman and Hill (2009), to work out solutions to their own situation and context through generating practical ideas to implement and then question each other to develop further insight. Participants were then challenged to take action and encouraged to develop an individual action plan.

### Measures

Intervention was a categorical variable indicating when the questions were answered: before the workshop intervention or after. The variable was coded as an indicator variable with 0 = before, 1 = after.

Mind-State upon arriving home was measured by participants providing a response to the question: When you arrive home how would you normally describe your state of mind? Respondents could choose from fourteen suggested options or alternatively describe their state of mind in their own words. The words used for the suggested options were adapted from those tested in the COPAS scale by Gilbert, McEwan, Mitra, Franks, Richter and Rockliff (2008) and from words assessed by Strauss and Allen (2008) as negative, neutral or positive. Sheldon and Lyubormirsky (2006) also suggest the use of 'quieter' positive emotion words, such as 'content', 'satisfied' and 'serene', and a selection of these words were added to the options. Phrases such as 'focus on work' or 'focus on family' were included. Whilst mind states can be transient states and vary in relation to work and home situations (e.g. Xanthopoulou, Bakker, & Ilies, 2012), the options were framed around participants' perceived normal mind-state on arrival at home. For analysis the responses were classified as Positive (e.g. relaxed; focused on the family), Neutral (e.g. indifferent) or Negative (e.g. agitated; focused on work) and a then recoded with Positive = 1, Neutral = 0, Negative = -1.

Work-Family Balance was measured using the scale of Carlson, Grzywacz and Zivnuska (2009). This comprises 6 questions all measured on a 5 point scale from Always (= 5) to Never (= 1). An example is: "I am able to negotiate what is expected of me at work and in my family".

Demographic variables shown in Table 2 above were included in the analysis as controls.

## Results

Summary measures of most of the variables are shown in Tables 1 and 2 above. Table 3 presents the covariance matrix for all the variables.

| Variable | Mean Pre | Mean Post | 1 | 2 | 3 | 4 | 5 | 6 | 7 | 8 |
|---|---|---|---|---|---|---|---|---|---|---|
| 1. Intervention | | | 0.45 | | | | | | | |
| 2. Mind-State | -0.29 | -0.05 | 0.13 | 0.79 | | | | | | |
| 3. WFB | 3.92 | 4.04 | 0.10 | 0.24 | 0.51 | | | | | |
| 4. Age | | | -0.01 | 0.11 | 0.10 | 10.8 | | | | |
| 5. Gender | | | 0.00 | -0.03 | -0.16 | -0.11 | 0.38 | | | |
| 6. Family status | | | 0.03 | 0.01 | 0.05 | -0.02 | -0.05 | 0.28 | | |
| 7. Work status | | | -0.05 | 0.11 | 0.16 | 0.10 | -0.21 | 0.09 | 0.41 | |

| Variable | Mean | 1 | 2 | 3 | 4 | 5 | 6 | 7 | 8 |
|---|---|---|---|---|---|---|---|---|---|
| 8. Work category | | -0.01 | 0.05 | 0.27 | 0.09 | -0.40 | 0.08 | 0.26 | 0.47 |

Table 3: Means, standard deviations and correlations

Two simple linear regressions were used to estimate the path coefficients for the model pictured in Figure 1. Figure 3 presents the estimated unstandardised regression coefficients for the regressions.

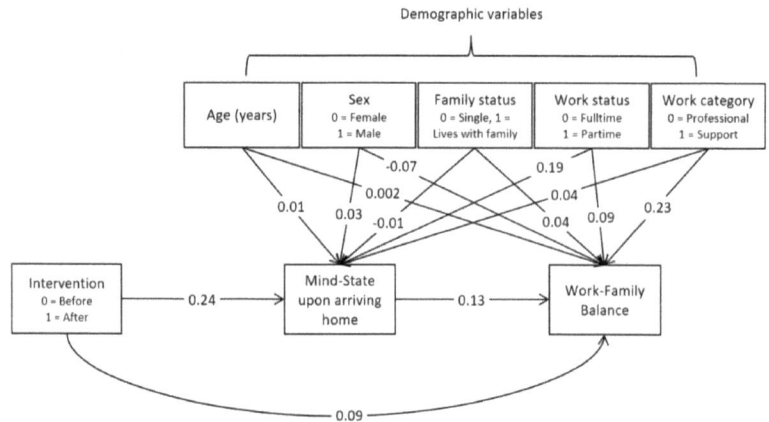

Fig. 3: Estimated unstandardised regression coefficients for the regressions

As noted previously only descriptive statistics can be used with this data; inferential statistical techniques are not appropriate. In particular, with the current design it is not possible to conclude if the population values of the various parameters differ from zero using statistical techniques. However, the results suggest the action learning intervention had effects; these are supported by qualitative comments, as discussed below.

The estimated coefficient for the Intervention term in the regression for Mind-State shows that the effect of the intervention was to increase Mind-State by 0.24 on average, from 0.29 to -0.05 (RQ1). However, Cohen's d is 0.30, so the effect size not large according to the rules of thumb noted by Cohen (1988).

We note in passing that the regression coefficients for the effects on Mind-State of two of the control variables, Age and Work Status, were positive, suggesting that older people and people employed part-time have a more positive Mind-State. This is related to research by Zacher, Jimmieson and Bordia (2014) that older workers had higher job satisfaction and lower emotional exhaustion at work.

The regression coefficient for the effect of Mind-State on Work-Family Balance was 0.13 (RQ2). The regression coefficient for the direct effect of Intervention on Work-Family Balance was also positive. The overall resulting effect of the Intervention on Work-Family Balance as shown in Table 3 was to increase the Work-Family Balance score by 0.12, from 3.92 to 4.04. This corresponds to a Cohen's d of 0.23.

We again note in passing that the regression coefficients for the effects of Work Status and Work Category on Work-Family Balance were positive, suggesting that people employed part-time and employees who work in a support, as opposed to a professional, role enjoy a more positive WFB. The findings relating to part-time work is in line with the summary research of Higgins, Duxbury and Johnson (2000). In relation to the complexity of different work types, studies have previously related this to their impact on negative spillover into the home (Grotto & Lyness, 2010) and work-family conflict (Dierdorff & Ellington, 2008).

Descriptive comments were optional in the post-workshop survey, however 58 participants responded, with 40 (approximately 5%) indicating that they had made a positive change, 13 indicating no change and 5 (less than 1%) indicating a negative change. All of the participants who indicated a negative change also mentioned changed family situations, such as illness or some crisis.

A summary of the positive change comments listed against the types of techniques participants had implemented is presented in Table 4. These comments add weight to the findings in relation to RQ1 in that individuals developed changed mind states on arrival at home. Specifically, 'Being present for their partner', an important mind-state on arrival at home, was identified by 23 participants as a technique they had implemented. An example comment is "When I am with my family I am much more present with them". 'Relaxation' was noted by 8 participants as a technique they had implemented. An example comment is "Used to feel drained but now relaxing more". 'Reflection/self-awareness' was noted by 12 participants as a technique they had implemented. An example comment is "When I am on the bus, I picture that I am leaving work at work". 'Read/play music on journey' was noted by 4 participants as a technique they had implemented. An example comment is "Put music on more often than news talk". 'Reduce work interruptions' was noted by 12 participants as a technique they had implemented. An example comment is "I rarely take work home. It helps me keep these boundaries". 'Sport or exercise' was noted by 5 participants as a technique they had implemented. An example comment is "After exercising I feel much more relaxed". In particular these comments indicate that some participants have initiated changes in their transition states, consistent with the intent of the intervention and in line Rotondo and Kincaid's (2008) findings about the influence of positive thinking. Other comments indicate that a number of participants were experiencing improved home arrangements and reduced work-life interference, consistent with Byron (2005) and Kreiner et al.'s (2009) recommendations relating to several coping mechanisms.

| Category of transition technique | Participants | Examples of comments |
|---|---|---|
| Being 'present' for partner | 23 | *Trying to be more focused on greeting with love and care when I get home* <br> *When I am with my family I am much more present with them* |
| Relaxation | 8 | *Used to feel drained but now am relaxing more* |
| Reflection / self-awareness | 12 | *When I am on the bus, I picture that I am leaving work at work* <br> *I try to switch off from work a lot more now and concentrate on home* |
| Read / play music on journey | 4 | *Put music on more often than news talk* |

| | | |
|---|---|---|
| Reduce work interruptions | 12 | *I rarely take work home. It helps me to keep these boundaries* <br> *I turn off the phone and just spend time with them* |
| Sport or exercise | 5 | *After exercising I feel much more relaxed* |

Table 4: Analysis of positive qualitative comments

## Discussion

The results suggest that the action learning intervention investigated in this study is likely to have made a positive difference for many workshop participants when they arrived at home. More specifically, the results suggest an impact of the intervention on the mind-state of participants when they arrived home, which in turn positively affected perceptions of WFB. These results suggest that action learning interventions like this one, based on exposing participants to positive psychological techniques such as mindfulness, are likely to affect the mind-state of participants who choose to utilize the techniques, and consequently lead to improved WFB.

Anonymity prevented the research study from tracking individual participants during the study, but it appears that many decided to try the techniques to which they were exposed. The overall scores for both mind-state and WFB increased, indicating that a number of participants made changes. The qualitative comments from participants such as those in Table 4, provide examples of the types of changes participants made to improve their mind-state on arrival from home. The changes are related to ideas discussed in the workshop. In particular, some adopted ideas associated with being 'present'. This is an important technique that individuals can use to cover up an underlying mood through the recognized practice of 'surface acting' (Grandey, 2003). 'Showing up' in a purposeful manner to their partner and children (such as in greeting them with love and care) is a decision made by the individual based on a reflection on mentally putting aside the work day (such as the Third Space technique of Rest, Reflect,

Reset), and concentrating on how they want to show up for the family.

Although statistical significance could not be assessed, the direct relationship between the mind-state and WFB was positive, as proposed. This aligns with similar findings of Michel et al. (2014), where an intervention led to improved work-life balance and reduced work-life conflict. However, by including mind-state as a mediator between the intervention and WFB our work suggests a possible mechanism by which interventions such as the one in this study may act. Further research is needed to more firmly establish any causal links, however, because the workshop included segmentation techniques that may also have directly contributed to the sense of improved WFB (e.g. see Kossek et al. (2012) where boundary controls had a negative relationship to work-family conflict).

As explained previously, the workshop focused on participants' use of the transition time between work and home. Participants mentioned activities such as listening to music and/or sport or exercise during this time. This approach differs from the approach used in some other training interventions around mindfulness: For example, the intervention studied in Josefsson et al. (2014) mostly consisted of training in meditation techniques while at work whereas that in Bono, Glomb, Shen, Kim and Koch (2013) employed positive reflection while at work. Focussing on the transition time may lead to participants being more likely to take tangible actions that may help clarify boundaries between roles (Kossek et al., 1999). This aligns with work of Ashforth et al. (2000); activities during transitions may help people to enter subsequent roles in a more positive psychological state.

Focusing on the transition time between work and home may also allow participants to select from a range of suggested techniques. Participants may, for example, choose techniques that they find most useful to their own situation. This choice is important as Wang, Repetti and Campos (2011) found that individuals have different coping mechanisms in relation to negative spillover, so offering a single 'solution' may not be effective.

The findings have implications for theory in WFB. In particular, they add to the literature on psychological detachment (Etzion et al., 1998) by identifying an additional process that may elicit detachment behavior. The research suggests that there is a link between the intervention and action that is mediated by mind-state, and that mind-state may be altered in a positive way in some workers by exposing them to ideas from positive psychology specifically targeted to the transition period between work and home.

The findings also have implications for human resource practice. As the workshop was designed and conducted by the third author (a practitioner), this study responds to the call by Kossek, Lewis and Hammer (2010) for research involving partnerships with practitioners in discovering best practices in work-life research. We note that The Third Space has already been utilised by many organisations in Australia and New Zealand to help employees to improve their work-family balance.

## Limitations and suggestions for future research

There are some limitations to this research. Due to the anonymous nature of the responses, the research was not able to track the changes to individual participants' responses, but instead relied mostly on results for the participants overall. Using this design it is impossible to assess the statistical significance of the regression coefficients or determine the proportion of participants who made a change as a result of the workshop from the quantitative data; the qualitative data from participant responses to the optional open-ended question tells us that at least 5% of the participants made a positive change. Further research is needed to determine the extent to which the results from this preliminary study can be generalised. Further research is also needed to determine the proportion of people who do make a positive change, and to identify characteristics of this group of people. More importantly, further research is needed to determine characteristics of people who are unwilling or unable to make changes and to investigate other ways of helping such employees improve their WFB. This would include further work to understand the small proportion of participants who reported a negative change in response to the workshop. It is possible, for example, that some participants in this study may have had no incentive, motivation or reason to take 'on board' any suggestions because the workshops were instigated by organisations.

Another limitation is that participants who completed the second survey may have been more interested in taking on changes and therefore more likely to respond in the second survey than others. This is similar to limitations reported by Giannopoulos and Vella-Brodrick (2011), where their results also supported the effectiveness of positive interventions. As above, further research is needed to understand characteristics of workers who will make positive changes in response to a workshop like The Third Space, and those who will not or cannot.

The relatively short period of time between the workshop and the time of the follow-up survey is another limitation. Further research is needed to determine the extent to which new behaviours adopted by participants would be sustained over the long-term. A mixed-methods approach such as that implemented by Sørensen and Holman (2014) in assessing an intervention in improving employee wellbeing would be recommended for future research.

Finally, further research may be undertaken to assess alternative models for how interventions like The Third Space affect mind-state. For example, it would be interesting to test models that include variables to investigate possible effects of different industries and occupations or include interaction terms such as Intervention*Work Status and Intervention*Work Category in the research model for the regression for Mind-State. A model with such interaction terms could be used to test if the effect of the intervention on Mind-State is different for Part-time versus Full-time or Professional versus Support employees.

## Conclusion

This research has shown that an action learning intervention in which people are exposed to ideas from positive psychology and detachment may improve their transitions from work to home, impacting on their perceptions of WFB. It also suggests that a mechanism for such change might be via an effect on the mind-state of employees on arrival at home.

# References

Adler, N.E., Horowitz, M., Garcia, A. & Moyer, A. (1998). Additional validation of a scale to assess positive states of mind. *Psychosomatic Medicine*, 60(1), pp. 26-32.

Allen, N.J. & Meyer, J.P. (1990). The measurement and antecedents of affective, continuance and normative commitment to the organization. *Journal of Occupational Pscyhology*, 63(1), pp. 1-18.

Allen, T.D., Johnson, R.C., Saboe, K.N., Cho, E., Dumani, S. & Evans, S. (2012). Dispositional variables and work-family conflict: A meta-analysis. *Journal of Vocational Behavior*, 80(1), pp. 17-26.

Ashforth, B.E., Kreiner, G.E. & Fugate, M. (2000). All in a day's work: Boundaries and micro role transitions. *Academy of Management Review*, 25(3), pp. 472-491.

Bakker, A.B., Demerouti, E., Oerlemans, W. & Sonnentag, S. (2013). Workaholism and daily recovery: A day reconstruction study of leisure activities. *Journal of Organizational Behavior*, 34(1), pp. 87-107.

Bono, J.E., Glomb, T.M., Shen, W., Kim, E. & Koch, A.J. (2013). Building positive resources: Effects of positive events and positive reflection on work stress and health. *Academy of Management Journal*, 56(6), pp. 1601-1627.

Bosch, C., Sonnentag, S. & Pinck, A.S. (2018). What makes for a good break? A diary study on recovery experiences during lunch break. *Journal of Occupational and Organizational Psychology*, 91(1), pp. 134-157.

Britt, T.W., Crane, M., Hodson, S.E. & Adler, A.B. (2016). Effective and ineffective coping strategies in a low-autonomy work environment. *Journal of Occupational Health Psychology*, 21(2), pp. 154-168.

Byron, K. (2005). A meta-analytic review of work–family conflict and its antecedents. *Journal of Vocational Behavior*, 67(2), pp. 169-198.

Carlson, D.S., Grzywacz, J.G. & Zivnuska, S. (2009). Is work–family balance more than conflict and enrichment? *Human Relations*, 62(9), pp. 1459-1486.

Cegarra-Leiva, D., Sánchez-Vidal, M. & Cegarra-Navarro, J.G. (2012). Work life balance and the retention of managers in Spanish SMEs. The *International Journal of Human Resources Management*, 23(1), pp. 91-108.

Cohen, J. (1988). *Statistical power analysis for the behavioural sciences*, 2nd ed. New York, Academic Press.

Csikszentmihalyi, M. (1988). The flow experience and its significance for human psychology. In Csikszentmihalyi, M. & Csikszentmihalyi, I.S. (Eds.), *Optimal experience: Psychological studies of flow in consciousness*. Cambridge, Cambridge University Press, pp. 15-35.

Csikszentmihalyi, M. (1990). *Flow: The psychology of optimal experience*. New York, Harper and Row.

Csikszentmihalyi, M. (2003). *Good business, leadership, flow and the making of meaning*. New York, Penguin Putnam.

Cuddleback, G., Wilson, E., Orme, J.G. & Combs-Orme, T. (2004). Detecting and statistically correcting sample selection bias. *Journal of Social Service Research*, 30(3), pp. 19-33.

Daniel, S. & Sonnentag, S. (2014). Work to non-work enrichment: The mediating roles of positive affect and positive work reflection. *Work & Stress*, 28(1), pp. 49-66.

Demerouti, E., Bakker, A.B., Sonnentag, S. & Fullagar, C.J. (2012). Work-related flow and energy at work and at home: A study on the role of daily recovery. *Journal of Organizational Behavior*, 33(2), pp. 276-295.

Dierdorff, E.C. & Ellington, J.K. (2008). It's the nature of the work: Examining behavior-based sources of work-family conflict across occupations. *Journal of Applied Psychology*, 93(4), pp. 883-892.

Etzion, D., Eden, D. & Lapidot, Y. (1998). Relief from job stressors and burnout: Reserve service as a respite. Journal of Applied Psychology, 83(4), 577–585.

Fiksenbaum, L.M. (2014). Supportive work-family environments: implications for work-family conflict and well-being. The International *Journal of Human Resource Management*, 25(5), pp. 653-672.

Fraser, A. (2012). *The Third Space: Using life's little transitions to find balance and happiness*. North Sydney, William Heinemann.

Giannopoulos, V.L. & Vella-Brodrick, D.A. (2011). Effects of positive and orientations to happiness on subjective well-being. *The Journal of Positive Psychology*, 6(2), pp. 95-105.

Gilbert, P., McEwan, K., Mitra, R., Franks, L., Richter, A. & Rockliff, H. (2008). Feeling safe and content: A specific affect regulation system?

Relationship to depression, anxiety, stress, and self-criticism. *The Journal of Positive Psychology*, 3(3), pp. 182-191.

Goleman, D.J. & Schwartz, G.E. (1976). Meditation as an intervention in stress reactivity. *Journal of Consulting and Clinical Psychology*, 44, pp. 456-466.

Grandey, A.A. (2003). When 'the show must go on': Surface acting and deep acting as determinants of emotional exhaustion and peer-rated service delivery. *Academy of Management Journal*, 46(1), pp. 86-96.

Greenhaus, J.H. & Beutell, N.J. (1985). Sources of conflict between work and family roles. *Academy of Management Review*, 10(1), pp. 76-88.

Grotto, A.R. & Lyness, K.S. (2010). The costs of today's jobs: Job characteristics and organizational supports as antecedents of negative spillover. *Journal of Vocational Behavior*, 76(3), pp. 395-405.

Grzywacz, J.G. & Carlson, D.S. (2007). Conceptualizing work-family balance: Implications for practice and research. *Advances in Developing Human Resources*, 9(4), pp. 455-471.

Grzywacz, J.G. & Marks, N.F. (2000). Reconceptualizing the work-family interface: An ecological perspective on the correlates of positive and negative spillover between work and family. *Journal of Occupational Health Psychology*, 5(1), pp. 111-126.

Hahn, T.N. (1976). *The miracle of mindfulness*. Boston, Beacon Press.

Hamilton, R., Vohs, K.D., Sellier, A-L. & Meyvis, T. (2011). Being of two minds: Switching mindsets exhausts self-regulatory resources. *Organizational Behavior and Human Decision Processes*, 115, pp. 13-24.

Hammer, L.B., Kossek, E.E., Anger, W.K., Bodner, T. & Zimmerman, K.L. (2011). Clarifying work–family intervention processes: The roles of work–family conflict and family-supportive supervisor behaviors. *Journal of Applied Psychology*, 96(1), pp. 134-150.

Higgins, C., Duxbury, L. & Johnson, K.L. (2000). Part-time work for women: Does it really help balance work and family? *Human Resource Management*, 39(1), pp. 17-32.

Horowitz, M., Adler, N. & Kegeles, S. (1988). A scale for measuring the occurrence of positive states of mind: A preliminary report. *Psychosomatic Medicine*, 50(5), pp. 477-483.

Hyman, J., Scholarios, D. & Baldry, C. (2005). Getting on or getting by? Employee flexibility and coping strategies for home and work. *Work, Employment and Society*, 19(4), pp. 705-725.

Jain, S., Shapiro, S.L., Swanick, S., Roesch, S.C., Mills, P.J., Bell, I. & Schwartz, E.R. (2007). A randomized controlled trial of mindfulness meditation versus relaxation training: Effects on distress, positive states of mind, rumination, and distraction. *Annals of Behavioral Medicine*, 33(1), pp. 11-21.

Josefsson, T., Lindwall, M. & Bromberg, A.G. (2014). The effects of short-term mindfulness based intervention on self-reported mindfulness, decentering, executive attention, psychological health, and coping style. *Mindfulness*, 5(1), pp. 18-35.

Kabat-Zinn, J. (1994). *Wherever you go, there you are: Mindfulness meditation in everyday life*. New York, Hyperion.

Kabat-Zinn, J., Lipworth, L. & Burney, R. (1985). The clinical use of mindfulness meditation for the self-regulation of chronic pain. *Journal of Behavioral Medicine*, 8, pp. 163–190.

Kabat-Zinn, J., Massion, M.D., Kristeller, J., Peterson, L.G., Fletcher, K.E., Pbert, L. et al. (1992). Effectiveness of a meditation-based stress reduction program in the treatment of anxiety disorders. *American Journal of Psychiatry*, 149, pp. 936–943.

Kossek, E.E. (2016). Implementing organizational work-life interventions: Toward a triple bottom line. *Community, Work & Family*, 19(2), pp. 242-256.

Kossek, E.E., Lewis, S. & Hammer, L.B. (2010). Work–life initiatives and organizational change: Overcoming mixed messages to move from the margin to the mainstream. *Human Relations*, 63(1), pp. 3-19.

Kossek, E.E., Noe, R. & DeMarr, B. (1999). Work–family role synthesis: Individual, family and organizational determinants. *International Journal of Conflict Resolution*, 10(2), pp. 102–129.

Kossek, E.E., Ruderman, M.N., Braddy, P.W. & Hannum, K.H. (2012). Work-nonwork boundary management profiles: A person-centered approach. *Journal of Vocational Behavior*, 81(1), pp. 112-128.

Kreiner, G.E. (2006). Consequences of work-home segmentation or integration: A person-environment fit perspective. *Journal of Organizational Behaviour*, 27, pp. 485-507.

Kreiner, G.E., Hollensbe, E. & Sheep, M. (2009). Balancing borders and bridges: Negotiating the work–home interface via boundary work tactics. *Academy of Management Journal*, 52(4), pp. 704-730.

Leslie, L.M., King, E.B. & Clair, J.A. (2019). Work-life ideologies: The contextual basis and consequences of beliefs about work and life. *Academy of Management Review*, 44(1), pp. 72-98.

Maertz, C.P. & Boyar, S.L. (2011). Work-family conflict, enrichment, and balance under 'levels' and 'episodes' approaches. *Journal of Management*, 37(1), pp. 68-98.

Marquardt, M., Skipton Leonard, J., Freedman, A. & Hill, C. (2009). *Action Learning for Developing Leaders and Organizations*. Washington, D.C., APA.

McCarthy, A., Cleveland, J.N., Hunter, S. Darcy, C. & Grady, G. (2013). Employee work-life balance outcomes in Ireland: a multilevel investigation of supervisory support and perceived organizational support. *The International Journal of Human Resource Management*, 24(6), pp. 1257-1276.

Michel, A., Bosch, C. & Rexroth, M. (2014). Mindfulness as a cognitive-emotional segmentation strategy: An intervention promoting work-life balance. *Journal of Occupational and Organizational Psychology*, 87, pp. 733-754.

Moreno-Jiménez, B., Mayo, M., Sanz-Vergel, A.N., Geurts, S., Rodríguez-Muñoz, A. & Garros, E. (2009). Effects of work–family conflict on employees' well-being: The moderating role of recovery strategies. *Journal of Occupational Health Psychology*, 14(4), pp. 427–440.

Nippert-Eng, C. (1996). Calendars and keys: The classification of 'home' and 'work'. *Sociological Forum*, 11(3), pp. 563–582.

Olson-Buchanan, J.B. & Boswell, W.R. (2006). Blurring boundaries: Correlates of integration and segmentation between work and non-work. *Journal of Vocational Behavior*, 68(3), pp. 432–445.

Park, Y., Fritz, C. & Jex, S.M. (2011). Relationships between work-home segmentation and psychological detachment from work: The role of communication technology use at home. *Journal of Occupational Health Psychology*, 16(4), pp. 457-467.

Revans, R. (1982). *The Origins and Growth of Action Learning*. Bromley, UK, Chartwell Brant.

Revans, R. (2011), *ABC of Action Learning*. Farnham, UK, Gower.

Rotondo, D.M. & Kincaid, J.F. (2008). Conflict, facilitation, and individual coping styles across the work and family domains. *Journal of Managerial Psychology*, 23(5), pp. 484-506.

Sanz-Vergel, A.I., Demerouti, E., Bakker, A.B. & Moreno-Jiménez, B. (2011). Daily detachment from work and home: The moderating effect of role salience. *Human Relations*, 64(6), pp. 775-799.

Sanz-Vergel, A.I., Demerouti, E., Moreno-Jiménez, B. & Mayo, M. (2010). Work-family balance and energy: A day-level study on recovery conditions. *Journal of Vocational Behavior*, 76(1), pp. 118-130.

Sanz-Vergel, A.I., Rodríguez-Muñoz, A., Bakker, A.B. & Demerouti, E. (2012). The daily spillover and crossover of emotional labor: Faking emotions at work and at home. *Journal of Vocational Behavior*, 81(2), pp. 209-217.

Seligman, M.E.P. (1994). *What you can change and what you can't*. New York, Knopf.

Seligman, M.E.P. & Csikszentmihalyi, M. (2000). Positive psychology: An introduction. *American Psychologist*, 55(1), pp. 5-14.

Sheldon, K.M. & Lyubormirsky, S. (2006). How to increase and sustain positive emotion: The effects of expressing gratitude and visualizing best possible selves. *The Journal of Positive Psychology*, 1(2), pp. 73-82.

Sianoja, M., Syrek, C.J., de Bloom, J., Korpela, K. & Kinnunen, U. (2018). Enhancing daily well-being at work through lunchtime park walks and relaxation exercises: Recovery experiences as mediators. *Journal of Occupational Health Psychology*, 23(3), pp. 428-442.

Sonnentag, S. (2001). Work, recovery activities, and individual well-being: A diary study. *Journal of Occupational Health Psychology*, 6, pp. 196-210.

Sonnentag, S. (2012). Psychological detachment from work during leisure time: The benefits of mentally disengaging from work. *Current Directions in Psychological Science*, 21(2), pp. 114-118.

Sonnentag, S. & Bayer, U-V. (2005). Switching off mentally: Predictors and consequences of psychological detachment from work during off-job time. *Journal of Occupational Health Psychology*, 10(4), pp. 393-414.

Sonnentag, S., Binnewies, C. & Mojza, E.J. (2008). 'Did you have a nice evening?' A day-level study on recovery experiences, sleep, and affect. *Journal of Applied Psychology*, 93(3), pp. 674-684.

Sonnentag, S. & Fritz, C. (2007). The recovery experience questionnaire: Development and validation of a measure for assessing recuperation and unwinding from work. *Journal of Occupational Health Psychology*, 12(3), pp. 204-221.

Sonnentag, S. & Grant, A.M. (2012). Doing good at work feels good at home, but not right away: When and why perceived prosocial impact predicts positive affect. *Personnel Psychology*, 65(3), pp. 495-530.

Sonnentag, S., Kuttler, I. & Fritz, C. (2010). Job stressors, emotional exhaustion, and need for recovery: A multi-source study on the benefits of psychological detachment. *Journal of Vocational Behavior*, 76(3), pp. 355-365.

Sørensen, O.H. & Holman, D. (2014). A participative intervention to improve employee wellbeing in knowledge work jobs: A mixed-methods evaluation study. *Work & Stress*, 28(1), pp. 67-86.

Strauss, G.P. & Allen, D.N. (2008). Emotional intensity and categorisation ratings for emotional and nonemotional words. *Cognition and Emotion*, 22(1), pp. 114-133.

ten Brummelhuis, L.L. & Bakker, A.B. (2012). Staying engaged during the week: The effect of off-job activities on next day work engagement. *Journal of Occupational Health Psychology*, 17(4), pp. 445-455.

Van Wijhe, C.I., Peeters, M.C.W. & Schaufeli, W.B. (2011). To stop or not to stop, that's the question: About persistence and mood of workaholics and work engaged employees. *International Journal of Behavioral Medicine*, 18, pp. 361-372.

Wang, S., Repetti, R.L. & Campos, B. (2011). Job stress and family social behavior: The moderating role of neuroticism. *Journal of Occupational Health Psychology*, 16(4), pp. 441-456.

Wayne, J.H., Butts, M.M., Casper, W.J. & Allen, T.D. (2017). In search of balance: A conceptual and empirical integration of multiple meanings and work-family balance. *Personnel Psychology*, 70(1), pp. 167-210.

Xanthopoulou, D., Bakker, A.B. & Ilies, R. (2012). Everyday working life: Explaining within-person fluctuations in employee well-being. *Human Relations*, 65(9), pp. 1051-1069.

Zacher, H., Jimmieson, N.L. & Bordia, P. (2014). Time pressure and co-worker support mediate the curvilinear relationship between age and occupational wellbeing. *Journal of Occupational Health Psychology*, 19(4), pp. 462-475.

Zheng, C., Kashi, K., Fan, D., Molineux, J, & Ee, M.S. (2016). Impact of individual coping strategies and organizational work-life balance programmes on Australian employee well-being. *The International Journal of Human Resource Management*, 27(5), pp. 501-526.

# Biographies

Dr John Molineux is a Senior Lecturer in the Department of Management at Deakin Business School and an AHRI Fellow Chartered Professional in Human Resources. John joined Deakin in 2010 after over 30 years in human resource management. He is currently teaching HRM and leadership to postgraduate students. His research interests focus on industry-sponsored projects, with an emphasis on human performance and wellbeing. John is also keenly interested in strategic HRM, organisation change and action research. In his previous career, he worked in HR roles in several organisations as an HR manager/director, HR strategist and other HR professional roles. He completed his PhD in 2005 which was an action research project that developed a systemic approach to Strategic HRM and resulted in organisational cultural change.

Dr Rodney Carr is a former academic from the Department of Management at Deakin University and is now semi-retired, but continues a relationship with Deakin University as a research associate. He is a former Director of Teaching and Learning and has a background in mathematics and statistics.

Dr Adam Fraser completed a PhD at the University of Wollongong and is a peak performance researcher who helps people strive to achieve better performance in everything they do. In his time he has worked with elite athletes and sporting teams, special forces soldiers and business leaders. He has written a number of books, including 'The Third Space' and 'Strive' and is in demand as a consultant, workshop facilitator and keynote speaker. What is unique about his research is that it focuses on how do people go beyond their potential without the collateral damage that normally comes with elite performance.

# Improving self-learning and dealing with adjustment challenges through individual reflective action research of an international MBA student

Tanya Ahmed

**Abstract**

*This study explores the improvements in self-learning and dealing with adjustment challenges in the life of an MBA student through individual reflective action research. I use individual reflective action research as the methodology, in other words, the first-person inquiry, which has encouraged me to ask questions about my practice and to work out the answers for myself. I continuously engage in self-reflective process on my practice to effect required changes. I chose action research as it allowed me to conduct this study within a compatible framework with my own professional integrity and values system. I believe that one can engage action research to bring out the best in one's life. The plethora of adjustment challenges typically faced by international students could be highlight. The study would also help international students to enhance their self-learning and acclimatize to new challenges in a foreign land.*

*I decided to include my faculties, classmates, group mates and husband in this study with myself being at its centre as a researcher. As a result, action research has led to increased knowledge for myself, my school and my fellow foreign classmates by describing the difficulties I had to come across and the steps that were taken to overcome them. I depicted the process of learning about my inner self, reflected on my actions, revised my concerns and adjusted my personal and social needs. These in turn assisted me to fathom and assess my own educational and personal advancement.*

**Key words:** Self-reflective process, adjustment challenges, self-learning, international students' challenges

| |
|---|
| **What is known about the topic?** |
| International students often face numerous difficulties when trying to acclimate themselves to a new culture. Research reveals that foreign students usually experience isolation and wistfulness at a higher pace particularly during their first year as opposed to their resident counterparts. |
| **What does this paper add?** |
| The plethora of adjustment challenges typically faced by international students could be highlight and how to handle them |
| **Who will benefit from its content?** |
| The study would also help international students to enhance their self-learning and acclimatize to new challenges in a foreign land |
| **What is the relevance to AL and AR scholars and practitioners?** |
| Action research can led to increased knowledge for scholars and practitioners by describing and analyzing the difficulties they had to come across and the steps that were taken to overcome them. Practitioners can learn more about their inner self, reflect on actions, revise their concerns and adjust their personal and social needs |

*Received  July 2020        Reviewed  October 2020        Published  December 2020*

# Introduction

This action research study explores the improvements in self-learning and dealing with adjustment challenges in the life of an MBA student through individual reflective action research. Various challenges confront international students and their attempts to accustomize themselves to a new environment. Research indicates that international students in general face loneliness and homesickness at a higher rate during their first year in comparison to their resident counterparts (Andrade, 2006). The implementation of the process of action research can assist in combating the new challenges faced by these students. Engaging in a self-reflective action research process can help to discover a better apprentice within ourselves. In order to do so, I narrate all my personal experiences and provide my insights on the lessons learned throughout the MBA program as an international student.

The application of specific frameworks helps to better understand the entire reflective action research.

It has always been my aspiration to acquire knowledge and broaden the prospects in life, which was the underlying reason behind my enrollment in the MBA program at De La Salle University (DLSU). During the program I learned and embraced specific frameworks in the action research class and fathomed the art of transforming theory into practice. One of the key eruditions is how to deal with various hurdles and habituate rather quickly to changing circumstances.

I went to Manila, Philippines, as part of my husband's job relocation in a multinational company. On a personal level, it was a novel experience for me to move to a foreign country.

## What is action research?

Reason and Bradbury (2008) indicate that action research's history is pervasive and has been in use by many social researchers to evaluate the functional issues jointly in wartime circumstances in both Europe and America. In the past, the main researcher often held control from the outset; however, the recent phenomenon encourages all the participants to be an integral part of the process so that each can benefit from it (Reason & Bradbury, 2008). Basically, the benefits of action research are not only confined to any individual rather it can be reaped by all as a team.

Action research is often regarded as an effective tool for self-assessment. McNiff (2002, p. 6) appropriately captures this in the declaration that "action research is an enquiry conducted by the self into the self".

Bradbury (2015) mention that action research provides relevant and realistic information, which proves to be useful for people in their regular lives. He further add that this application of knowledge could positively impact the economic, legal and mental health of the people and the community as a whole. Hence, it is not conducted simply for the sake of conducting research rather it provides a more practical outcome which can be beneficial for everyone. Bradbury (2015) suggests that in order to gather knowledge, a democratic and participatory orientation is essential in action research, which would help to find appropriate solutions to various issues in collaboration with all the members in the team.

Action research is unique in the sense that it demands some sort of self-intervention unlike conventional research that frowns on interference in the research setup (Kemmis, 1982). Figure 1 depicts an action research cycle.

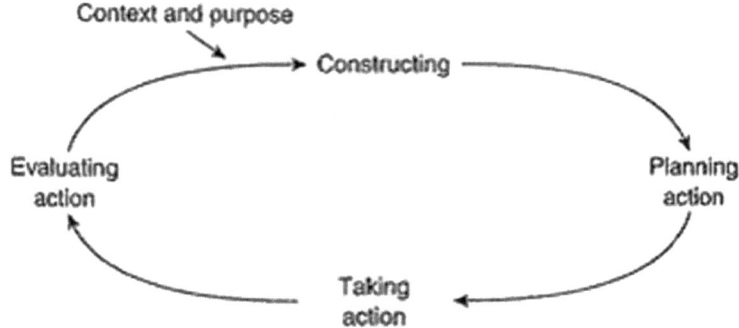

Figure 1: The action research cycle (Coghlan & Brannick, 2014, p. 9)

This cycle of activities forms an action research spiral in which each cycle increases the researchers' knowledge of the original question, puzzle or problem hoping that it will lead to a solution. The concept of inquiring can be accomplished using the first, second and third-person dimensions (Torbert, 1998, 2000). Marshall and Mead (2005) explain that research or practice techniques and strategies in first person intervention address the researcher's capacity to cultivate an inquisitive attitude to his or her own life, to act with preference and consideration, and to evaluate results in the real environment while operating. They further add that the process of first person observation formulates the research into more of our moments of action, not as external researchers, but in the entire context of daily activities.

The second-person study continues with interpersonal communication and entails the growth of research groups and learning organizations (Reason & Bradbury, 2008). The second-person intervention addresses the opportunity to inquire face-to-face with others about issues of common interest such as strengthening personal and technical practice independently and separately (Marshall & Mead, 2005). The third-person action research encourages and promotes extensive involvement of all the participants' inquest over time, for instance, in an organization (Coghlan & Brannick, 2014) or a geographic region, as established in the Scandinavian action research tradition with its increased focus on endorsing democratic process (e.g., Gustavsen, 2001). Furthermore, the third-person action research has the ability to influence and transform public sentiment, corporate strategy, government policy and so on, but "through mutuality-enhancing exercises of power that invite third-persons into first, second, and third person research/practice" (Reason & Torbert, 2001, p. 23).

## Literature review

Reflective action has long been part of many great transformative practices, from Buddhism (Goldstein, 1983) to Jesuit (Coghlan, 2004) philosophical exercises, the method of analyzing one's own actions and learning about oneself. Vaccarino et al. (2006) maintain that as it includes professionals, action research is also referred to as practitioner-based research and is often known as self-reflective practice as it engages people or professionals focusing on their own work.

The self-reflection methodology is a crucial part of action research. Concurrently, activity researchers would not only examine the lives of others; rather they would also draw attention to their own functioning as researchers. Hargreaves and Daw (1990) indicate that although it is hard to explain self-reflection, the decision as an outcome of that would actually be insightful and the learning from it will be fruitful. A reflective practice involves a consistent and thoughtful analysis of values and behaviors and an awareness of the reasoning behind and the aftermath of particular behavior (Dewey, 1933; Schon, 1983).

Given the literature of reflective practice, it is noteworthy to mention that this is a beneficial approach used for many years because of its ability to make us reflect on our own actions.

## Adjustment issues faced by international students

The difficulties and barriers faced by foreign students enrolling into higher education institutions have been discussed in several reports. These challenges include, but are not limited to, language difficulties, cultural changes and various other hurdles in communication with the staffs and peers. Additionally, these students experience fatigue, anxiety, feelings of alienation, differing social interactions, cultural shock, financial struggles, lack of sufficient accommodation, solitude and loneliness, among others (Bradley, 2000, Erichsen & Bolliger, 2011, Lee & Rice, 2007).

Rosenthal, Russell and Thomson (2008), who researched 979 international students attending an Australian metropolitan university discovered that due to lack of information about services, students were underutilizing both health and counseling services and were uncomfortable in availing those services. Psychological disorders, i.e. depression, fretfulness, dejection, etc. are common among them (Sam, 2001). International students are also hospitalized more frequently compared to native students (Mitchell, Greenwood & Guglielmi, 2007). This indicates that it is not only the social alienation that international students have to put up with, rather, there are health concerns as well. Other complexities include seclusion, lack of support, limited relationship with locals, new methods of learning, a changing sense of identity, impractical expectation of family, disturbance at home country, unpleasant incident in the host country and estrangement (Deakins, 2009; Hanassab, 2006; Klomegah, 2006; Leask, 2009; McClure, 2007; Mitchell et al., 2007; Neri & Ville, 2007; Rosenthal et al., 2008).

Campbell and Li (2008) surveyed 22 Asian students at a New Zealand university. Their study revealed major obstacles such as untried methods of interaction in a classroom setup being uninformed about academic norms and rules, insufficient support for learning, problems developing interpersonal relationships with local students and lacking a sense of belongingness.

Robertson et al. (2000) conducted a study on the interactions of university personnel with foreign students. The results revealed that due to the students' lack of language proficiency, the employees were not compassionate enough towards the overseas students, but they were blamed for not excelling in their academic performance. Walter (2004) points out that in English speaking nations, East Asian students typically encounter language barriers because of the considerable disparity between their native language and culture with those of the host nation.

Liu (2012), a Chinese researcher who went to Canada as an international student concluded that in her graduate level courses she came across immense intricacies in interpreting the conversation among her peers and even the lecturers. She also had trouble addressing daily issues such as getting the right transportation, shopping for groceries or calling for assistance. Therefore, it is imperative to note that beside several other issues, one of the major hurdles that international students face is the inability to speak and understand the native language in the host country. Beoku-Betts (2004) revealed an interesting observation about overseas students, i.e. they are susceptible to racism and stereotypes, hence this is one of the most major concerns that need to be addressed by the educational institution from the outset.

International students are burdened with the tasks of managing their own accommodation, selecting the right banks for transfer of funds and commuting with local transports like taxis and buses in a completely unknown territory. Sustaining in a new culture is often one of the first lessons that they need to cope with. International students also undergo a major cultural clash after their relocation to a new country (Wu, Garza & Guzman, 2015). On the contrary, a differing view was presented by Severiens and

Wolff (2008) that those international students who adapt to the new environment with ease maintain good liaison with their instructors and peers and engage in extracurricular activities are more likely to sustain in school and accomplish their desirable level of success.

Hence, by taking into account the various aforementioned literatures, it can be concluded that there is a substantial cultural gap between the native and foreign students. This cultural stress causes a number of detrimental effects on foreign students (Constantine, Okazaki & Utsey, 2004).

The literature has noted, for example, that the problems encountered by foreign students frequently cause feelings of uneasiness, uncertainty, depression, anxiety, stress, language complexities, feelings of inferiority, difficulties in adapting to new food and cultural values, lack of care, perceived prejudice and homesickness.

## Research questions

This first-person action research addresses the following research questions:

1. How can self-reflective action research unveil a better learner in ourselves?

2. What adaptation obstacles are faced by international students?

3. How are these obstacles addressed through individual reflective action research?

## Research methodology

The first-person inquiry provides a fundamental practice and disciplines of our intervention analysis process from which we can track the effect of our actions (Marshall & Mead, 2005). In modern social science, reflective practice is also known as 'first-person research' (Marshall & Mead, 2005). Schon (1983) asserts that a "reflective practitioner" is an individual who enthusiastically makes him- or herself the subject of a study in order to enhance professional practice through a process of self-reflection.

The first-person research 'upstream' methodologies include autobiographical writing, psychology, meditation, defensive arts and other disciplines that build perception, consciousness and appearance in motion (Houston, 1982), use of artwork (Booth, 1997), sensory awareness (Brooks, 1974) and several others. The first-person 'downstream' research or practice may require insightful analysis of day-to-day behavior, building on characteristics of building on characteristics of knowledge and self-control to objectively note the effect of one's actions in the broader world and the congruence or incongruence of one's behavior with the goals or concepts (Argyris & Schon, 1994). The first-person action research has paved the way for me to get implicated in my own research, addressing the issues of concern to me which have arisen within my practice, with the intention to make further improvements. It requires a lot of commitment and determination from "me", the practitioner, to investigate and reflect honestly and critically on my own practice. My research offers a description of and an explanation for my own professional learning. It has also given me the prospect to attend to all the issues while drawing on my own experience.

The methodology of action research is a self-reflective process where one is constantly evaluating what one is doing, evaluating solutions and self-evaluation with a view to make further advancement in the quality of life through taking time to reflect on what is happening and how to change it.

## Story and outcome

My story began back in May of 2012. I received a late call from DLSU and was given the confirmation that I was selected for the MBA program. Subsequently, I commenced the program with lots of enthusiasm along with a certain degree of apprehension as well. Leadership, Ethics and CSR was my first ever MBA course. From the onset when I first entered the classroom, I was rather prompt to comprehend that it was indeed a momentous occasion for me and was on course for something big ahead. On a personal level, it would not have been possible for me to take up the MBA program without the incessant support of my husband and the family as a whole. Interestingly enough, I discovered that I was the only foreigner in the class during the introduction. My other peers were either undergraduates from De La Salle or from other academic institutions in the Philippines. Until that point, I had no friends in the Philippines at all. And I was somewhat jittery as well in initiating a conversation with unknown people in completely new surroundings.

As a part of this course, one of the partial provisions was to serve any organization and assist them in their mission for a given period of time. I went to the Servants of Jesus Community Foundation, Inc. (SOJCFI) with my group mates. Even though I belong to a different religion, it did not discourage me in lending a helping hand for this foundation. Both my honor and humanity were elevated by the whole experience. This was a field job, which really enabled me to learn and realize that there is nothing in this world that can give you more pleasure than the self-satisfaction of helping the less fortunate people in the community. I compared the educational system between the Philippines and my home country Bangladesh during the course of the MBA program. I found that the educational system in Bangladesh is mostly adopted from the British curriculum and style of teaching. In my undergraduate school (in Bangladesh), we were more motivated to study the ideas rather than put it into practice. In general, we (Bangladeshis) are very good at memorizing, but not so effective at applying it in real life. I felt this perspective in my MBA to be something unique where we need to focus more in the application of the ideas and frameworks rather than just memorizing them.

During my stint at MBA School, one of the key balancing acts was to match the timing for my holidays to Bangladesh (as per the scheduled annual leave of my husband) with that of my semester break. More often than not, I had to undertake the additional burden of completing and submitting all my assignments ahead of the deadline. I had to request my mentors to allow a lot of my tests and assessments to be conducted online so that it could have been finished without my physical presence in the campus. There have also been incidents when I had to convince my group mates to make a presentation earlier than the due date because of my unavailability at the scheduled time.

I had undergone numerous adaptation problems by the end of the first term as I was still an alien to the whole system. Bradley (2000) and Ellis et al. (2005) found out that first of all, students who go to higher education have to adapt to the new environment. In addition, international students have several stressors such as language differences, cultural norms, detrimental psychological aspects, lack of support networks, etc. In Bangladesh, during my undergraduate studies, it was possible to devote enough time for both studies and work; however, it was not the case in the Philippines. Much of my time was occupied with other things and it was rather difficult to allocate the required time for studies. At the new school, there was certainly a lack of sense of belongingness; I experienced some linguistic problems and cultural gaps in addition to the academic concerns.

I could fathom that every institution has their different style of management and administration, but in my case as a DLSU student, there were instances of communication barriers due to language differences to a certain extent both in and outside the classroom (I sincerely believe it was not premeditated). There were quite a few cases where a lecturer would suddenly start delivering the lecture in Tagalog (Philippines National Language) with the presumption that all the students would be able to follow the lecture clearly. My group mates were more comfortable in discussing case studies in Tagalog, but later made me a part of it by summarizing it at the end.

Besides, at times I would be exhausted with many extra activities of little benefit, such as social networking, roaming around, testing out my culinary skills, etc. As a result, undoubtedly, I got deprived of a holistic growth and did not do full justice to my potential as an MBA student.

During the course of the MBA program I had the chance to interact with other international students in my university and learned about their adaptation challenges, most of which are actually common to many as depicted in this paper. They find it difficult to adjust to new social expectations and beliefs that often challenge them, gain academic achievement while encountering diverse and unfamiliar teaching and learning styles, and deal with homesickness and loneliness. Furthermore, as most foreign students are funded by private or family sources, they are likely to experience greater pressure to excel.

## Self-reflection and learning of the action researcher

Coghlan and Brannick (2014) explain that one of the most crucial parts of action research dissertation is to reflect on what knowledge we have acquired through intervening about ourselves and not just limiting it to the system that we are aiming to change.

A set of questions by Johns (2004) provided a model of structured reflection with some more useful questions to use when reflecting-in-action and on action. I contentedly used this for my intervention stage of action research:

- What would I do differently next time?
- What have I learned about myself from this experience?
- Could I avoid this situation another time?
- What other choices do I have?
- What would happen if I did nothing?
- What do I hope to achieve by doing that?
- What do I feel about this new information?
- How does it impact on me?
- What have I learned about myself?

My reflections are as follows:

- I understood that a lack of sense of belongingness in a new country is very natural as it takes time to adjust to a completely new backdrop.
- Establishing a proper daily routine and outlining the priorities is essential.
- Unfamiliar patterns of classroom interactions should not have limited me to explore new challenges in life.
- Struggles can help us to develop as competent individuals.
- An interaction between staff and faculty is a very vital concern for international students as they are the first with regards to whom we can evaluate and directly relate our experiences with the institution. Additionally, making friends and interacting with local students is important for survival. I wish I had the opportunity of peer tutoring programs in which my Filipino classmates would have assisted me but it did not happen much as most of them were full-time professionals.
- At times, I felt too much stressed out with studies because I was overloading myself with four courses each term. Instead of getting disappointed, I should have learnt to take criticisms and improve my performance to reach the ideal CGPA that I opted for. Instead of worrying about the failures, I should have celebrated success by recollecting some achievements.
- Throughout my MBA days, I was stressed and nervous as my family had high expectations for me to complete my studies with flying colors when it came to studies and particularly whether I was under pressure because of reaching deadlines, I think I should have been more coordinated, focused and forward thinking.

# Reflection on the story in the light of the experience and theory

Coghlan (2004) suggests that:
> if you are a participant in a Master's program engaging in classical action research, such as an action-oriented MBA program, you use frameworks to make sense of what is going on. You may be drawing on frameworks which help you make sense of an industry analysis, the performance of a firm and the like. Your use of frameworks aligns the story to the theory, and through this alignment you demonstrate your understanding of the theory and its application (p. 149).

Coghlan and Brannick (2014) provide the following questions as a guideline for using Schein's ORJI framework for reflective action research similar to my action research approach.

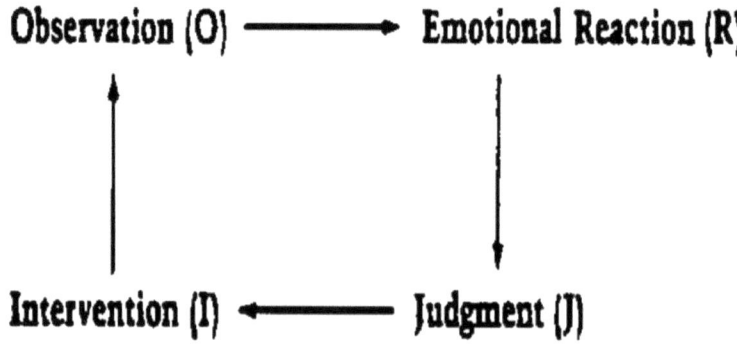

Figure 2: Intra-psychic process: The basic ORJI cycle (Schein, 1999, p. 87)

1. What did I actually observe? Can I describe it?

Observation: From the beginning of the first term, one of the key observations about me was that I did not value time. Instead of spending excessive time on social networking, wandering aimlessly, shopping, wasting time for long hours, I did not choose my time for value adding practices. I did not keep a proper schedule and refused to allocate enough time for each assignment. This seemed to cause many problems, especially when I had to reach a deadline. That is why, owing to my disposition of constantly having projects done at the eleventh hour, I suffered from enormous stress, which was somewhat upsetting for me and my family as well.

2. How did I react? What feelings were aroused in me?

Reaction: I did not acknowledge the fact that I often had to struggle for things to get it done until the very end. There was also a natural tendency to defend myself by saying that I had to take care of the family, do the usual household chores and all. What created the dilemma was the pattern of self-defending and denial, and I made it act as a protection for me, which would give me some respite at least. There were instances when I studied throughout the night before the start of the class to complete an assignment or a term paper. Although each and every time I reacted quite negatively to that practice of getting things done at the last minute, nevertheless I ended up doing the same thing over and over again ultimately.

3. What was my judgment about what happened? What thoughts or evaluations did the event trigger?

Judgment: I contemplated that this certain trait of mine needs to be worked on very carefully and smartly because if this was overlooked, there might be a time that I would have to pay the penalty for it on a bigger scale, which would eventually not only hurt me but also the people around me. In due course of time when I did realize that my quality of work was being hampered because of this peculiarity of doings things just in time for the deadline, it actually triggered me to intervene.

4. What did I do about it? How did I intervene?

Intervention: As there was so much of pressure of studies by taking 12 credits in a term, I kept a detailed calendar entry on my mobile phone and diary for all the courses and their due dates for submission of cases, assignments or presentations. I tried to finish and submit ahead of deadlines of a project, though was unable to attain it in some cases. In addition, I put notes on the walls of my room about the things I had to do. I even used the support of my husband by telling him to motivate me to do my pending activities as and when he saw me wasting my time or being inactive. I decided to divide my tasks in parts and even praised myself when I understood that I was able to finish a job efficiently on or before time and still have time for leisure activities.

To sum up, I used John's (2004) questions as a method to reflect on my actions. It was a successful strategy.

In order to further utilize the above reflections for personal virtue development, I additionally used means-ends analysis and reflection questions adopted from Alford and Naughton (2001).

Table 1: Reflections on actions

| Reflection component | Reflection question | My reflection |
| --- | --- | --- |
| END: What am I doing it for? | Is my personal motivation inherently good? Is the outcome I seek inherently good? Am I doing it for a good and for the common good? And not just for money or recognition? | My goal was to discover the different problems of adaptation faced by foreign students when they go to school in an unfamiliar land. In order to fix or strengthen it, I strived to find solutions about how to best cope with ethnic, social disparities and workload – by discussing a problem that I felt needed be discussed.<br><br>I followed this study not only for myself, but also for the good of many other international students like me at DLSU and for the university. |

| Reflection component | Reflection question | My reflection |
|---|---|---|
| ACTS (means): What am I doing? | Is my action plan proportionate to my end and respectful of human development? | It was beneficial to use self-assessment, journal keeping, using ORJI etc. as a way of action plan.<br><br>I continued to correspond and follow up with my supervisors and lecturers as to what challenges I had encountered.<br><br>They made a massive difference to find answers to a variety of issues.<br><br>In the process of achieving my goals, I have learned not to leap to conclusions or be hostile.<br><br>There have been times where I felt like giving up, then when I thought of the high expectations that everybody had from me, it helped me to reiterate again. |
| Circumstances: What are the particular circumstances? | Have I taken into account the history, present and future consequences of the act? | As I wrote the action study paper on this unique issue, I did take the history, current and future consequences into account. My question on how to strengthen self-learning by reading several other study papers and coping with adaptation problems has helped me to look deeper into it.<br><br>That would not have existed otherwise. I now recognize that this is a prevalent occurrence practically faced by every international student, but I also appreciate that there are avenues to solve it that will make studying a more enjoyable experience. |

My means-ends analysis indicated to me a reasonable link between pursuing a good end with good means.

# Extrapolation to a broader context and articulation of usable knowledge

Coghlan and Brannick (2014) explain that this section of action research would show the consequences of our reflection on the story and articulation of usable knowledge where we need to articulate how our research project can be extrapolated (or transported) to a wider context. These extrapolations would then answer the 'So what?' question in relation to our research.

Marshall and Reason's popular notion of three audiences of research suggests:

> All good research is for me, for us, and for them: it speaks to three audiences. It is for them to the extent that it produces some kind of generalizable ideas and outcomes...it is for us to the extent that it responds to concerns for our praxis, is relevant and timely..[for] those who are struggling with problems in their field of action. It is for me to the extent that the process and outcomes respond directly to the individual researcher's being-in-the-world (1994, pp. 112-113).

## The significance of this research for me

In undertaking this research, I conclude that as a foreign MBA student, I accomplished what I wanted to bring about a change in my educational practice in self-learning and coping with adaptation challenges. In my personal and professional growth, it was essential to reflect on my principles and evaluate my classroom practice in the light of those ideals. The reflective essence of action analysis has continually made me curious about "What am I doing?" and "How am I going to improve it?" The process is ongoing, and I can say with absolute certainty that I continue living my personal and professional life in this manner. It has led to the growth of my professional capacity and my sense of professional well-being. It has also given me the ability to clarify my educational principles, practice and skills.

In summary, this research was indeed a steep learning curve for me. Before this action study project, I had the impression that there is no need to research one self, but I now acknowledge that I can see what, where and how I can focus on improving myself with self-evaluation.

It gave me the courage to believe that I was in refutation and I also figured out how to improve a situation through self-reflection. Action research has tapped into my life and encouraged me to unleash the potential inside me, the buoyant force of assurance that there is nothing I cannot achieve if I believe in myself. It inspired me, made me more accountable for my learning, and gave me a chance to see that if one genuinely wants to achieve something, nothing can stop them.

I have learned that making time to celebrate my strengths and working on my weaknesses has been invaluable to my self-esteem. It has increased my consciousness that I have to continuously remind myself of the uniqueness I have and the beautiful things I have to give to the world, no matter how substantial or insignificant it might be. I see developments in my interpersonal relationships, sharing ideas, reflecting critically and honestly looking at my work and being my own judge. I am now beginning to value the freedom of stopping and reflecting, questioning, and exploring my own responses.

Once again, I became a practitioner, trying to analyze my practice, taking ownership of my successes and inadequacies, focusing on a coherent and organized way on strategies to enhance myself. It was an exciting and worthwhile experience to carry out this piece of research on a concerning issue.

## The significance of this research for us and for them

This research would get others interested in it as well even though they were not directly involved as they can understand how international students can work as a team by fostering and building on qualities of support, trust and openness between teachers, staff and students. Gebhard (2012) points that while foreign students definitely ought to make an effort to adjust themselves, he doesn't want to put all the blame for cultural integration on them. Teachers and school administrators can help understand how foreign students feel and take a closer look at their adaptation process, such as making international students socialize with local students more frequently, speaking in a shared language, and offering accommodative lectures, and so on. I was emotionally encouraged by few of my faculty members who helped me to gather enough confidence to pursue my degree. If you can give people inspiration when coping with a single situation, if you can explain a realistic approach to them, then the problem can be solved. I strongly believe that this research project has helped to positively impact my future practice.

I consider that action research might well be a much more feasible choice for individuals involved, as it helps individuals in their own educational settings to innovate and handle progress. With others' help, I have claimed awareness that I have enhanced the educational experience level for myself and my other fellow foreign classmates.

Using action research, an international student like me can contribute to this and understand how to evaluate their vulnerabilities and strengths. They should be confident that they are not the only ones having transition problems, but their seniors have already gone through this process and came out of it successfully.

## Conclusion

For me, a foreign MBA student's experience was an overwhelming one. I will always recall these two years of my life amid certain struggles. I have learned how to question my own beliefs and assumptions now. To boost one's self-learning is never very late, and it is not difficult to cope with problems either. Every day is a new beginning to do something remarkable, so we need to have the strength to see it transform into reality. The process of contemplation should have begun much earlier, which would have made me more mindful of the deficiencies I wanted to fix and the strengths I should have reflected on.

Teehankee (2018) points out that the goal of the implementation of action research focused on critical pragmatic science theory was to enable the MBA graduates of the university to become reflexive and humanistic agents of change in their working contexts by applying evaluation, critical thinking, collaborative analysis, and action and academic skills. I can reassure after these two years of exposure to my MBA that I can share my thoughts freely and more confidently. This new shift in me would undoubtedly assist me as a practitioner in the future as well, where I will still be a strong communicator by listening to the opinions of other people.

I have been encouraged to be a thoughtful lifelong learner after all these years of learning in which I can focus on every part of life, explore a more profound sense of my work, challenge and have a better holistic understanding of the entire process itself.

## References

Alford, H. J., & Naughton, M. J. (2001). *Managing as if faith mattered*. Notre Dame, IN: University of Notre Dame.

Andrade, M. S. (2006) International students in English-speaking universities: Adjustment factors. *Journal of Research in International Education*, 5(2), pp. 131-154.

Argyris, C. & Schon, D. (1994) Theory into practice: Increasing professional effectiveness. *Behavioral Science*, 39(3), pp. 254-256.

Beoku-Betts, J. (2004). African women pursuing graduate studies in the sciences: Racism, gender bias, and third world marginality. *NWSA Journal*, pp. 116-135.

Booth, E. (1997) *The everyday work of art: How artistic experience can transform your life*. Naperville, IL: Sourcebooks.

Bradbury, H. (Ed.). (2015). *The SAGE handbook of action research*. London: Sage. Doi: 10.4135/9781473921290.

Bradley, G. (2000) Responding effectively to the mental health needs of international students. *Higher Education*, 39(4), pp. 417-433.

Brooks, C. V. W. (1974) *Sensory awareness: The rediscovery of experiencing*. Santa Barbara, CA: Ross-Erikson Publishers.

Campbell, J., & Li, M. (2008) Asian students' voices: An empirical study of Asian students' learning experiences at a New Zealand university. *Journal of Studies in International Education*, 12(4), pp. 375-396.

Coghlan, D. (2004) Seeking God in all things: Ignatian spirituality as action research. *The Way*, 43(1), pp. 1-14.

Coghlan, D., & Brannick, T. (2014). *Doing action research in your own organization* (4th ed.). Los Angeles: SAGE.

Constantine, M. G., Okazaki, S., & Utsey, S. O. (2004) Self-concealment, social self-efficacy, acculturative stress and depression in African, Asian and Latin American international college students. *American Journal of Orthopsychiatry*, 74(3), pp. 230-241.

Deakins, E. (2009) Helping students value cultural diversity through research-based teaching. *Higher Education Research & Development*, 28(2), pp. 209-226.

Dewey, J. (1933) *How we think*. Chicago: Henry Regnery.

Ellis, B., Sawyer, J., Gill, R., Medlin, J., & Wilson, D. (2005) Influences of the learning environment of a regional university campus on its international graduates. *Australian Educational Researcher*, 32(2), pp. 65-85.

Erichsen, E. A., & Bolliger, D. U. (2011) Towards understanding international graduate student isolation in traditional and online environments. *Educational Technology Research and Development*, 59(3), pp. 309-326.

Gebhard, J. G. (2012) International students' adjustment problems and behaviors. *Journal of International Students*, 2(2), pp. 184-193.

Goldstein, J. (1983) *The experience of insight: A simple and direct guide to Buddhist meditation*. Boulder, CO: Shambhala.

Gustavsen, B. (2001). Theory and practice: The mediating discourse. In P. Reason & H. Bradbury (Eds.), *The Sage handbook of action research. Participative inquiry and practice* (2nd ed.). London: Sage.

Hanassab, S. (2006) Diversity, international students and perceived discrimination: Implications for educators and counselors. *Journal of Studies in International Education*, 10(2), pp. 157-172.

Hargreaves, A., & Daw, R. (1990). Paths of professional development: Contrived collegiality, collaborative culture and the case of peer coaching. *Teaching and Teacher Education*, 6, pp. 227-241.

Houston, J. (1982 *The possible human*. Los Angeles: J.P. Tarcher.

Johns, C. (2004) *Becoming a reflective practitioner*. (2nd ed.). Oxford: Blackwell.

Kemmis, S. (Ed.). (1982) *The action research reader*. Geelong, Victoria: Deakin University Press.

Klomegah, R. Y. (2006) Social factors relating to alienation experienced by international students in the United States. *College Student Journal*, 40(2), pp. 303-315.

Leask, B. (2009) Using formal and informal curricula to improve interactions between home and international students. *Journal of Studies in International Education*, 13(2), pp. 205-221.

Lee, J. J., & Rice, C. (2007) Welcome to America? International student perceptions of discrimination. *Higher Education: The International Journal of Higher Education and Educational Planning*, 53(3), pp. 381-409.

Liu, L. (2012) An international graduate student's ESL learning experience beyond the classroom. *TESL Canada Journal*, 29(1), pp. 77-92.

Marshall, J., & Mead, G. (2005) Self-reflective practice and first-person action research. *Action Research*, 3(4), pp. 233-332.

Marshall, J., & Reason, P. (1994) Adult learning in collaborative action research: Reflections on the supervision process. *Studies in Continuing Education: Research and Scholarship in Adult Education*, 15(2), pp. 117-132.

McClure, J. W. (2007) International graduates' cross-cultural adjustment: Experiences, coping strategies and suggested programmatic responses. *Teaching in Higher Education*, 12(2), pp. 199-217.

McNiff, J. (2002). *Action research for professional development: Concise advice for new action researchers*. Dorset: September Books.

Mitchell, S. L., Greenwood, A. K., & Guglielmi, M. C. (2007). Utilization of counseling services: Comparing international and US college students. *Journal of College Counseling*, 10(2), pp. 117-129.

Neri, F. & Ville, S. (2008) Social capital renewal and the academic performance of international students in Australia. *The Journal of Socio-Economics*, 37, pp. 1515-1538.

Reason, P., & Bradbury, H. (2008) Introduction. In Reason, P. & Bradbury, H. (Eds). *The Sage handbook of action research* (2nd ed.). London, U.K.: Sage, pp. 1-13.

Reason, P., & Torbert, W.R. (2001) The action turn: Toward a transformational social science. *Concepts and Transformations*, 6(1), pp. 1-37.

Robertson, M., Line, M., Jones, S., & Thomas, S. (2000). International students, learning environments and perceptions: A case study using the Delphi technique. *Higher Education Research & Development*, 19(1), pp. 89-102.

Rosenthal, D. A., Russell, J., & Thomson, G. (2008) The health and well-being of international students at an Australian university. *Higher Education: The International Journal of Higher Education and Educational Planning*, 55(1), pp. 51-67.

Sam, D. (2001) Satisfaction with life among international students: An exploratory study. *Social Indicators Research*, 53(3), pp. 315-337.

Schein, E. (1999) *Process consultation revisited: Building the helping relationship*. Reading, MA: Addison-Wesley.

Schon, D. (1983) *The reflective practitioner: How professionals think in action*. New York: Basic Books.

Severiens, S., & Wolff, R. (2008) A comparison of ethnic minority and majority students: Social and academic integration and quality of learning. *Studies in Higher Education*, 33(3), pp. 253-266.

Teehankee, B. (2018) Critical realist action research and humanistic management education. *Humanistic Management Journal*, 3(1), pp. 1-20.

Torbert, W. (1998) Developing courage and wisdom in organizing and sciencing. In S. Srivastva, & D. Cooperrider (Eds). *Organizational wisdom and executive courage*. San Francisco: The New Lexington Press, pp. 222-253.

Torbert, W. R. (2000). Transforming social science: Integrating quantitative, qualitative, and action research. In *Transforming social inquiry, transforming social action*. Springer, Boston, MA, pp. 67-91.

Vaccarino, F., Comrie, M., Culligan, N., & Sligo, F. (2006) *Action research initiatives: The Wanganui adult literacy and employment programme*. Palmerston North: Massey University.

Walter, T. (2004) *Teaching English language learners: The how-to handbook*. White Plains, NY: Longman.

Wu, H. P., Garza, E., & Guzman, N. (2015). International students' challenge and adjustment to college. *Education Research International* 2015, 1–9. doi: 10.1155/2015/202753

# Biography

Tanya Ahmed is a Lecturer, teaching Management and Business Communication at the School of Business and Economics, North South University, Bangladesh. She received her Masters of Business Administration from De La Salle University, Philippines. Her professional experience includes teaching virtually to Japanese students.

Ahmed has a passion for teaching in both online and offline platforms. Her research interests lie in Social Entrepreneurship, Organizational Behavior, SME's, and Human Resource Management.

She has also served as a Faculty Advisor for a student club at North South University. She is always looking for opportunities to increase her depth of knowledge.

# Membership information and article submissions

## Membership categories

Membership of Action Learning, Action Research Association Ltd (ALARA) takes two forms: individual and organisational.

### ALARA individual membership

Members of the ALARA obtain access to all issues of the *Action Learning and Action Research Journal* (*ALARj*) twelve months before it becomes available to the public.

ALARA members receive regular emailed Action Learning and Action Research updates and access to web-based networks, discounts on conference/seminar registrations, and an on-line membership directory. The directory has details of members with information about interests as well as the ability to contact them.

### ALARA organisational membership

ALARA is keen to make connections between people and activities in all strands, streams and variants associated with our paradigm. Areas include Action Learning, Action Research, process management, collaborative inquiry facilitation, systems thinking, Indigenous research and organisational learning and development. ALARA may appeal to people working at all levels in any kind of organisational, community, workplace or other practice setting.

ALARA invites organisational memberships with university schools, public sector units, corporate and Medium to Small Business, and community organisations. Such memberships include Affiliates. Details are on our membership link on our website (https://alarassociation.org/membership/Affiliates).

# Become a member of ALARA

An individual Membership Application Form is on the last page of this Journal or individuals can join by clicking on the Membership Application button on ALARA's website. Organisations can apply by using the organisational membership application form on ALARA's website.

## For more information on ALARA activities and to join

Please visit our web page:
https://www.alarassociation.org/user/register
or email admin@alarassociation.org

## Journal submissions criteria and review process

The *ALARj* contains substantial articles, project reports, information about activities, creative works from the Action Learning and Action Research field, reflections on seminars and conferences, short articles related to the theory and practice of Action Learning and Action Research, and reviews of recent publications. *ALARj* also advertises practitioners' services for a fee.

The *ALARj* aims to be of the highest standard of writing from the field in order to extend the boundaries of theorisation of the practice, as well as the boundaries of its application.

ALARA aims *ALARj* to be accessible for readers and contributors while not compromising the need for sophistication that complex situations require. We encourage experienced practitioners and scholars to contribute, while being willing to publish new practitioners as a way of developing the field, and introduce novice practitioners presenting creative and insightful work

We will only receive articles that have been proof read, comply with the submission guidelines as identified on *ALARj*'s website, and that meet the criteria that the reviewers use. We are unlikely to publish an article that describes a project simply because its methodology is drawn from our field.

ALARA intends *ALARj* to provide high quality works for practitioners and funding bodies to use in the commissioning of works, and the progression of and inclusion of action research and action learning concepts and practices in policy and operations.

*ALARj* has a substantial international panel of experienced Action Learning and Action Research scholars and practitioners who offer double blind and transparent reviews at the request of the author.

*Making your submission and developing your paper*

Please send all contributions in Microsoft Word format to the Open Journal Systems (OJS) access portal: https://alarj.alarassociation.org

You must register as an author to upload your document and work through the four electronic pages of requirements to make your submission. ALARA's Managing Editor or Issue Editor will contact you and you can track progress of your paper on the OJS page.

If you have any difficulties or inquiries about submission or any other matters to do with ALARA publications contact the Managing Editor on editor@alarassociation.org.

For the full details of submitting to the *ALAR Journal*, please see the submission guidelines on ALARA's web site https://alarassociation.org/publications/submission-guidelines/alarj-submission-guidelines.

*Guidelines*

*ALARj* is devoted to the communication of the theory and practice of Action Learning, Action Research and related methodologies generally. As with all ALARA activities, all streams of work across all disciplines are welcome. These areas include Action Learning, Action Research, Participatory Action Research, systems thinking, inquiry process-facilitation, process management, and all the associated post-modern epistemologies and methods such as rural self-appraisal, auto-ethnography, appreciative inquiry, most significant change, open space technology, etc.

In reviewing submitted papers, our reviewers use the following criteria, which are important for authors to consider:

Criterion 1: How well are the paper and its focus both aimed at and/or grounded in the world of practice?

Criterion 2: How well are the paper and/or its subject explicitly and actively participative: research with, for and by people rather than on people?

Criterion 3: How well do the paper and/or its subject draw on a wide range of ways of knowing (including intuitive, experiential, presentational as well as conceptual) and link these appropriately to form theory of and in practices (praxis)?

Criterion 4: How well does the paper address questions that are of significance to the flourishing of human community and the more-than-human world as related to the foreseeable future?

Criterion 5: How well does the paper consider the ethics of research practice for this and multiple generations?

Criterion 6: How well does the paper and/or its subject aim to leave some lasting capacity amongst those involved, encompassing first, second and third person perspectives?

Criterion 7: How well do the paper and its subject offer critical insights into and critical reflections on the research and inquiry process?

Criteria 8: How well does the paper openly acknowledge there are culturally distinctive approaches to Action Research and Action Learning and seek to make explicit their own assumptions about non-Western/ Indigenous and Western approaches to Action Research and Action Learning

Criteria 9: How well does the paper engage the context of research with systemic thinking and practices

Criterion 10: How well do the paper and/or its subject progress AR and AL in the field (research, community, business, education or otherwise)?

Criterion 11: How well is the paper written?

*Article preparation*

*ALARj* submissions must be original and unpublished work suitable for an international audience and not under review by any other publisher or journal. No payment is associated with submissions. Copyright of published works remains with the author(s) shared with Action Learning, Action Research Association Ltd

While *ALARj* promotes established practice and related discourse *ALARj* also encourages unconventional approaches to reflecting on practice including poetry, artworks and other forms of creative expression that can in some instances progress the field more appropriately than academic forms of writing.

Submissions are uploaded to our Open Journal System (OJS) editing and publication site.

The reviewers use the OJS system to send authors feedback within a 2-3 month period. You will receive emails at each stage of the process with feedback, and if needed, instructions included in the email about how to make revisions and resubmit.

*Access to the journal*

The journal is published electronically on the OJS website.

EBSCO and InformIT also publish the journal commercially for worldwide access, and pdf or printed versions are available from various online booksellers or email admin@alarassociation.org.

For further information about the ALAR Journal and other ALARA publications, please see ALARA's web site http://www.alarassociation.org/publications.

# Individual Membership Application Form

This form is for the use of individuals wishing to join ALARA.
Please complete all fields.

## Name

| Title | Given Name | | Family Name |
|---|---|---|---|

## Residential Address

| Street | | Town / City | Postcode / Zip |
|---|---|---|---|
| Country | | | |

## Postal Address

| Street | | Town / City | Postcode / Zip |
|---|---|---|---|
| State | | Country | |

## Telephone / Mobile Telephone

| Country Code | Telephone Number | Country Code | Mobile Number |
|---|---|---|---|

## Email

Email Address

## Experience (Please tick most relevant)

- ☐ No experience yet
- ☐ 1 – 5 years' experience
- ☐ More than 5 years' experience

## Interests (Please tick all relevant)

- ☐ Education
- ☐ Health
- ☐ Community / Social Justice
- ☐ Indigenous Issues
- ☐ Gender Issues
- ☐ Organizational Development

## Are you eligible for concessional membership?

If you are a full-time student, retired or an individual earning less than AUD 20,000 per year; about USD 13,750 (please check current conversion rates), you can apply for concessional membership.

## Do you belong to an organization that is an Organizational Member of ALARA?

If you are a member of such an organization, you can apply for the Reduced Membership Fee. Please state the name of the Organizational Member of ALARA in the box below.

## Payment

We offer a range of payment options. Details are provided on the Tax Invoice that we will send to you on receipt of your membership application.

POST billpay | BPAY | MasterCard | VISA

If you want to join and pay online, please go to https://www.alarassociation.org and click on the Membership Application button (lower right). Alternatively, please complete and return this form to us.

**By Post**
ALARA Membership
PO Box 162 Greenslopes
Queensland 4120
AUSTRALIA

**By FAX**
+ 61 (7) 3342 1669

**By Email**
admin@alarassociation.org

## Annual Membership Fees (Please select one)

| Full Membership | | Concessional Membership | |
|---|---|---|---|
| ☐ AUD 143.00 | Developed Country | AUD 71.50 | ☐ |
| ☐ AUD 99.00 | Emerging Country | AUD 49.50 | ☐ |
| ☐ AUD 55.00 | Developing Country | AUD 27.50 | ☐ |

| Reduced Membership Fee, as I belong to an Organizational Member of ALARA | Developed | AUD 71.50 | ☐ |
|---|---|---|---|
| | Emerging | AUD 49.50 | ☐ |
| | Developing | AUD 27.50 | ☐ |

Organization's name: _____

## Privacy Policy

By submitting this membership form, I acknowledge that I have read, understood and accept ALARA's Privacy Policy https://www.alarassociation.org/sites/default/files/docs/policies/ALARA_PrivacyPolicy11_1.pdf.

ALARA will acknowledge receipt of your application and send you an invoice or receipt of payment. You will receive an email confirming activation of your account, and details on how you can access website functions.

*ALARA is a global network of programs, institutions, professionals, and people interested in using action learning and action research to generate collaborative learning, training, research and action to transform workplaces, schools, colleges, universities, communities, voluntary organisations, governments and businesses.*

*ALARA's vision is to create a more equitable, just, joyful, productive, peaceful and sustainable society by promoting local and global change through the wide use of Action Learning and Action Research by individuals, groups and organisations.*

Printed by Libri Plureos GmbH in Hamburg, Germany